# STUMPED

## WOMEN'S CRICKET PUZZLES

Stephen Hearn

STUMPED Book of Cricket Puzzles
First published in 2024



Published by Stumped Cricket
www.stumpedcricket.com

Cover design and illustrations by Stephen Hearn
All puzzles devised and created by Stephen Hearn

ISBN: 978 1739213817

# INTRODUCTION

Hello and welcome to *STUMPED Women's Cricket Puzzles*.

If, like me, you're a fan of women's international cricket and enjoy solving puzzles, then you'll love this book. It's a totally unique collection of fantastic puzzles and word games designed to test your knowledge of women's cricket. Featuring crosswords, logic problems, brainteasers, and loads more, it's guaranteed to provide you with endless hours of fun and give your brain cells a great workout.

The collection of puzzles feature over 500 past and present women's cricketers from around the world in a variety of problems specifically designed to provide just the right level of challenge, brain gymnastics and quiet satisfaction. Yes, this book really does feature over 500 women's international cricketers – and from 40 different nations. Don't worry if you struggle to name more than a handful of women's cricketers at present. *STUMPED* is more of a test of your puzzle-solving skills than your ability to name lots of cricketers.

You'll find the challenges includes familiar, classic puzzle types – many of which you can solve within a short break. And a few other puzzles that may be new to you and will stretch your brain cells a little further. I suggest you complete the puzzles using a soft pencil, and with an eraser close at hand, just in case you need to correct any mistakes!

The puzzles come thick and fast – starting with the image on the front cover and the women's international cricket teams displayed on the stumps. Three of the teams have yet to play a Women's Test match and have therefore only ever played white-ball cricket. Can you name the three teams? Well done if you can – but if you can't, I guarantee that by the end of this book you'll be better placed to solve the brainteaser. And I don't just mean by looking at the answers in the Solutions section!!

The challenges are also guaranteed to sharpen your puzzle-solving skills and open a gateway to a host of therapeutic benefits for mental health and overall wellbeing. Research shows that tackling puzzles on a regular basis can improve cognitive functions such as memory, concentration and vocabulary, as well enhance problem-solving and critical thinking skills. Word games are also a great way to relax, relieve stress and unwind after a long day.

So, what better way to achieve these benefits and at the same time have lots of fun – than to test your knowledge and puzzle-solving skills with the world of women's international cricket.

*Stephen Hearn*

Note: Unlesss otherwise stated, the information contained in *STUMPED* is accurate as of 20 October 2024 at the conclusion of the ICC Women's T20 World Cup 2024.

## FIELDING POSITIONS 1

Can you correctly match-up the cricket fielding positions?

| | |
|---|---|
| EXTRA | LEG |
| LONG | POINT |
| SQUARE | CORNER |
| THIRD | MID-WICKET |
| SILLY | MAN |
| FLY | COVER |
| BACKWARD | HIT |
| DEEP | MID-ON |
| COW | SLIP |
| STRAIGHT | OFF |

## ROTATION 2

Find the starting point and fill in the blanks to reveal the name (7,9) of an India women's cricketer (*104 WT20I's, 2018-24*). Only alternate letters are shown.

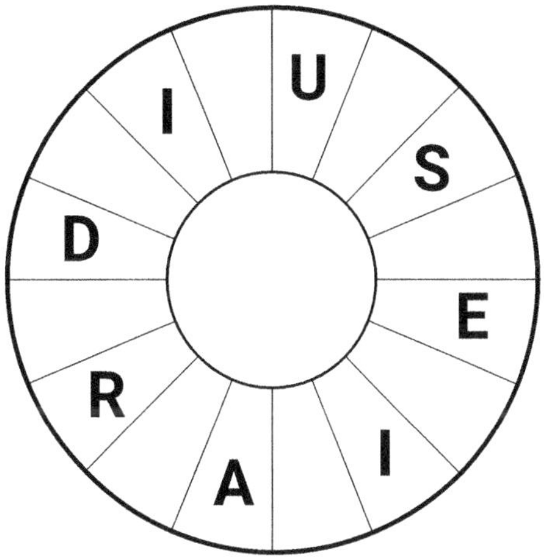


## CRIDOKU 3

Fill in the squares of the grid so that each row, each column and each smaller 3x3 block contains all the letters which spell **GABY LEWIS** (IRE) (*91 WT20I's, 2014-24*) only once.

| | | | | | | | | |
|---|---|---|---|---|---|---|---|---|
| | I | | | W | | | B | |
| S | | | I | | L | | | E |
| B | | | | | | | | S |
| G | | B | | L | | S | | Y |
| | | E | | | | A | | |
| I | | A | | G | | B | | L |
| A | | | | | | | | I |
| W | | | Y | | A | | | G |
| | L | | | S | | | A | |

## CONNECTION 4

Can you sort the 16 past and present women's international cricketers into four connecting groups of 4 and identify what connects the groups. For example you might think that Bryce, Green, Kerr and Sokomanu were all born in South Africa or have a surname that is also a colour.

Note: Some cricketers may fall into more than one group but they only belong in one complete group of four.

| | | | |
|---|---|---|---|
| Joyce (AUS)<br>**BATH** | Johanna (VAN)<br>**SOKOMANU** | Jean (NZ)<br>**STONELL** | Manal (BAH)<br>**MALIK** |
| Sabbhineni (IND)<br>**MEGHANA** | Amy (ENG)<br>**JONES** | Kayleen (NAM)<br>**GREEN** | Jess (NZ)<br>**KERR** |
| Catherine (IRE)<br>**O'NEILL** | Alex (AUS)<br>**BLACKWELL** | Jacqueline (ENG)<br>**COURT** | Beth (AUS)<br>**MOONEY** |
| Kathryn (SCO)<br>**BRYCE** | Juliet (NED)<br>**POST** | Mehreen (HK)<br>**YOUSAF** | Isobel (IRE)<br>**JOYCE** |

## BUMP BALL 5

Can you identify the missing letters that complete the surnames of 5 South Africa women's cricketers?
Next, rearrange the missing letters to spell the surname of another South Africa women's cricketer (*75 WODI's, 2010-24*).

| | | | | |
|---|---|---|---|---|
| M | L | A | B | |
| B | O | | C | H |
| J | | F | T | A |
| | E | W | I | S |
| K | H | A | | A |

## RECORD HOLDER 6

Nia Charlotte Greig is the youngest international cricketer of all time - both male or female.

Nia set the record on 31 July 2019 playing for Jersey Women against France Women in the Women's T20I Quadrangular Series. France won the match by 7 wickets. How old was Nia?

A. 11 years, 40 days
B. 12 years, 293 days
C. 13 years, 6 days
D. 14 years, 364 days

# WORDSEARCH



The surnames of the 22 cricketers who played in the first women's Test match, contested between Australia and England in December 1934, are hidden in the Wordsearch below. The names can be found written horizontally (forwards and backwards), vertically (up or down) or diagonally. Can you find them?

| | | | | | | | | | | | | | | | |
|---|---|---|---|---|---|---|---|---|---|---|---|---|---|---|---|
| U | T | R | E | D | S | O | R | I | N | B | T | V | A | T | G |
| E | S | A | L | O | R | K | E | T | T | E | L | S | P | N | E |
| D | O | E | Y | W | D | A | N | X | K | V | M | A | U | G | A |
| N | Y | P | A | L | M | P | R | T | A | S | L | R | D | I | H |
| L | A | S | I | T | O | A | U | L | N | M | A | I | S | E | U |
| L | M | H | Y | B | N | R | T | O | E | I | R | O | H | I | P |
| I | C | E | G | L | A | G | W | R | O | T | C | L | G | C | N |
| V | L | D | R | A | H | C | T | I | R | P | H | N | T | H | A |
| E | A | N | T | O | N | S | N | A | L | I | D | O | I | U | G |
| H | R | L | I | P | U | O | P | Y | T | R | A | L | C | M | A |
| S | E | W | E | C | T | S | M | F | C | O | L | M | A | E | L |
| K | B | D | R | N | D | Q | I | T | Y | S | E | Z | H | P | C |
| A | E | V | A | H | T | A | V | R | I | C | A | D | T | O | A |
| N | I | J | Y | R | L | I | E | B | E | R | T | H | I | E | M |
| H | L | L | A | B | W | O | N | S | O | A | P | E | M | H | K |
| E | B | P | T | S | N | V | R | E | M | N | H | U | S | W | C |

**AUSTRALIA Women**

**ANTONIO** Peggy (AUS, *1934-37*)
**BLADE** Fernie (AUS, *1934*)
**HILLS** Hilda (wkt) (AUS, *1934*)
**KETTELS** Lorna (AUS, *1934-35*)
**MCLARTY** Nell (AUS, *1934-37*)
**MONAGHAN** Ruby (AUS, *1934-35*)
**PALMER** Anne (AUS, *1934-35*)
**PEDEN** Margaret (Capt.) (*1934-37*)
**PRITCHARD** Hazel (AUS, *1934-37*)
**SHEVILL** Essie (AUS, *1934-35*)
**SMITH** Kath (AUS, *1934-37*)

**ENGLAND Women**

**ARCHDALE** Betty (Capt.) (*1934-37*)
**CHILD** Mollie (ENG, *1934-37*)
**HIDE** Molly (ENG, *1934-54*)
**LIEBERT** Joy (ENG, *1934-35*)
**MACLAGAN** Myrtle (ENG, *1934-51*)
**PARTRIDGE** Joy (ENG, *1934-35*)
**SNOWBALL** Betty (wkt) (*1934-49*)
**SPEAR** Mary (ENG, *1934-35*)
**TAYLOR** Peter (ENG, *1934-37*)
**TURNER** Doris (ENG, *1934-35*)
**VALENTINE** Carol (ENG, *1934*)

# CRYPTOGRAM

**8**

A quote by England captain Heather Knight (*143 WODI's, 2010-24*) about an opposing player has been encrypted by replacing each letter of the alphabet with another. We've started to decipher the quote but can you finish it off and also reveal who Heather was talking about?

| G | C | H | | C | X | G | | A | C | H | | X | F | P | O | P | A | D | | A | Y |
|---|---|---|---|---|---|---|---|---|---|---|---|---|---|---|---|---|---|---|---|---|---|
| | | | | | | | | | | | | | B | | | | | | | | |

| J | O | P | N | U | | X | | G | S | P | A | N | C | | X | T | W | | C | P | A |
|---|---|---|---|---|---|---|---|---|---|---|---|---|---|---|---|---|---|---|---|---|---|
| | | | | | | | | | | | | | | | | | | | | | |

| A | C | H | | F | X | O | O | | S | C | H | E | H | I | H | E | | G | C | H | |
|---|---|---|---|---|---|---|---|---|---|---|---|---|---|---|---|---|---|---|---|---|---|
| | | | | B | | | | | | | | R | | | | R | | | | | |

| S | X | T | A | G | . | | G | A | X | J | X | T | P | H | | A | X | D | O | Y | E |
|---|---|---|---|---|---|---|---|---|---|---|---|---|---|---|---|---|---|---|---|---|---|
| | | | | | . | | | | | | | | | | | | | | | | R |

# HIT FOR SIX

**9**

Complete the grid so that every row and column, and every outlined area, contains each of the letters found in the surname of Alice **CAPSEY** (ENG) (*37 WT20I's, 2022-24*).

| A | | | | | |
|---|---|---|---|---|---|
| | C | | | S | |
| | | | | | E |
| | | Y | | | |
| | | | | | |
| | | | P | | |

# BATTING ORDER

**10**

Can you rearrange the boxes of the grid below to spell the name of a women's international cricketer *(106 WT20I's, 2009-24)*?

| ES | PR | HI |
|---|---|---|
| AB | HA | OD |
| NI | UD | KA |

# CRICKET CODEWORD



Each number in the grid represents a different letter of the alphabet. Can you complete the grid correctly and identify the reference to women's international cricket in the shaded squares?

| 1 | 23 | 7 | 8 | 24 | 2 | 5 | ■ | 9 | 26 | 23 | 23 | 22 |
|---|---|---|---|---|---|---|---|---|---|---|---|---|
| 6 | ■ | 13 | ■ | 9 | ■ | 7 | ■ | 25 | ■ | 26 | ■ | 18 |
| 26 | 7 | 15 | 23 | 26 | ■ | 3 | 7 | 15 | 6 | 7 | 13 | 24 |
| 12 | ■ | 18 | ■ | 4 | ■ | 2 | ■ | 2 | ■ | 8 | ■ | 23 |
| 26 | 3 | 2 | 21 | 26 | 13 | 24 | ■ | 26 | 10 | 24 | 6 | 7 |
| 6 | ■ | 8 | ■ | ■ | ■ | 25 | ■ | 13 | ■ | ■ | ■ | 20 |
| ■ | 20 | 9 | 2 | 24 | 26 | ■ | 12 | 26 | 6 | 13 | 8 | ■ |
| 19 | ■ | ■ | ■ | 6 | ■ | 5 | ■ | ■ | ■ | 22 | ■ | 8 |
| 7 | 2 | 8 | 23 | 26 | ■ | 7 | 16 | 21 | 22 | 4 | 26 | 13 |
| 5 | ■ | 17 | ■ | 11 | ■ | 4 | ■ | 26 | ■ | 7 | ■ | 26 |
| 11 | 13 | 18 | 5 | 11 | 23 | 26 | ■ | 16 | 7 | 21 | 15 | 26 |
| 7 | ■ | 7 | ■ | 26 | ■ | 6 | ■ | 18 | ■ | 2 | ■ | 14 |
| 23 | 7 | 24 | 26 | 6 | ■ | 7 | 6 | 24 | 2 | 5 | 23 | 26 |

A B C D E F G H I J K L M N O P Q R S T U V W X Y Z

| 1 | 2 | 3 | 4 | 5 | 6 | 7 | 8 | 9 | 10 | 11 | 12 | 13 |
|---|---|---|---|---|---|---|---|---|---|---|---|---|
| 14 | 15 G | 16 | 17 | 18 | 19 | 20 | 21 | 22 O | 23 | 24 | 25 | 26 |

---

# CONUNDRUM



Can you unscramble the anagram to reveal the name of a Bangladesh women's cricketer?

**NATURAL GAINS** (BAN) (*103 WT20I's, 2015-24*)

# CROSS OVER

13

The answers in this puzzle are the names of the 50 women's international cricketers who have scored the highest number of runs in WODI matches. Can you complete the puzzle?

***3 LETTERS***
**LEE** Lizelle (SA) *3,315*
**RAJ** Mithali (IND) *7,805*

***4 LETTERS***
**KAPP** Marizanne (SA) *3,056*
**KAUR** Harmanpreet (IND) *3,565*
**KERR** Amelia (NZ) *2,082*
**LUUS** Sune (SA) *2,265*
**RAUT** Punam (IND) *2,299*
JAVERIA **KHAN** (PAK) *2,885*

***5 LETTERS***
**BATES** Suzie (NZ) *5,718*
**CLARK** Belinda (AUS) *4,844*
**DRUMM** Emily (NZ) *2,844*
**HEALY** Alyssa (AUS) *3,011*
**PERRY** Ellyse (AUS) *3,958*
**ROLLS** Rebecca (NZ) *2,201*

***6 LETTERS***
**BROWNE** Nicola (NZ) *2,002*
**CHETTY** Trisha (SA) *2,703*
**CHOPRA** Anjum (IND) *2,856*
**DEVINE** Sophie (NZ) *3,860*
**DOTTIN** Deandra (WI) *3,727*
**HAYNES** Rachael (AUS) *2,585*
**KNIGHT** Heather (ENG) *3,913*
BISMAH **MAROOF** (PAK) *3,369*
**MOONEY** Beth (AUS) *2,380*

**ROLTON** Karen (AUS) *4,814*
**SHARMA** Deepti (IND) *2,019*
**SHARMA** Jaya (IND) *2,091*
**TAYLOR** Claire (ENG) *4,101*
**TAYLOR** Sarah (ENG) *4,056*
**TAYLOR** Stafanie (WI) *5,691*
**TIFFEN** Haidee (NZ) *2,919*

*7 LETTERS*
**BRITTIN** Jan (ENG) *2,121*
**DU PREEZ** Mignon (SA) *3,760*
**EDWARDS** Charlotte (ENG) *5,992*
**HOCKLEY** Debbie (NZ) *4,064*
**LANNING** Meg (AUS) *4,602*

*8 LETTERS*
**BEAUMONT** Tammy (ENG) *4,094*
**GREENWAY** Lydia (ENG) *2,554*
**MANDHANA** Smriti (IND) *3,585*
**MATTHEWS** Hayley (WI) *2,434*
**NITSCHKE** Shelley (AUS) *2,047*

*9 LETTERS*
**BLACKWELL** Alex (AUS) *3,492*
**KEIGHTLEY** Lisa (AUS) *2,630*
**MCGLASHAN** Sara (NZ) *2,438*
**STHALEKAR** Lisa (AUS) *2,728*
**WOLVAARDT** Laura (SA) *4,148*

*10 LETTERS*
**VAN NIEKERK** Dane (SA) *2,175*

*11 LETTERS*
**ATHAPATHTHU** Chamari (SL) *3,713*
**SCIVER-BRUNT** Nat (ENG) *3,676*
**SIRIWARDENE** Shashikala (SL) *2,029*

*13 LETTERS*
**SATTERTHWAITE** Amy (NZ) *4,639*

# STEPLADDER 14

Climb from **JANE** at the bottom of the ladder to **SMIT** at the top by changing just one letter to form a word and without disturbing the order of the remaining letters. The clues are provided to help you out but are not in the correct order.

JANE SMIT is a former cricketer for England Women (*109 WODI's, 1993-2007*).

| SMIT |
| --- |
| |
| |
| |
| |
| |
| |
| JANE |

A country or state

Small grains of rock in desert

A narrow road

Moved smoothly along a surface

A long, narrow cut or opening

Something already mentioned

# BRAINTEASER 15

During a summer/winter season a total of 22 cricketers were selected to play for Australia Women in various fantasy fixtures against England, India, New Zealand and South Africa. Out of the 22 cricketers involved, 14 played in at least one Test match, 19 in a One Day International (WODI) and 17 in a Twenty20 International (WT20I).

What is the minimum number of cricketers that must have played in all three formats of the game?

# LOGIC PUZZLE



It's the start of a WODI match and Australia Women have set an attacking field for the opening over, with three slips alongside the wicket-keeper. From the information below can you identify where each player is fielding, as well as the number of WODI matches they have played and the cricket team they play for?

**Player:** Agnes, Harriet, Martha, Zoe
**WODI's:** 8, 21, 35, 64
**Cricket team:** New South Wales, Tasmania, Victoria, Western Australia

**Wicket-keeper** **1st slip** **2nd slip** **3rd slip**

Clues:

1. Zoe, who has featured in 21 WODI matches, plays for New South Wales.
2. The least experienced of the four players is fielding next to the cricketer who plays for Victoria.
3. Agnes, who has played 35 WODI matches, is not fielding at 1st slip.
4. The wicket-keeper is the most experienced of the four players.
5. Harriet, positioned at 3rd slip, does not play for Tasmania.

| PLAYER | FIELDING POSITION | WODI MATCHES | CRICKET TEAM |
|---|---|---|---|
| Agnes | | | |
| Harriet | | | |
| Martha | | | |
| Zoe | | | |

# WAGON WHEEL

**17**

How many words of four or more letters can you make from the letters on the wheel. Each word must include the central letter and other letters may only be used once. Plurals, foreign words and proper nouns are not eligible. See if you can find the nine letter word that is also the name of a cricket ground that has hosted women's international matches.

Target: 15 words = GOOD, 30 words = EXCELLENT, 45 words = OUTSTANDING

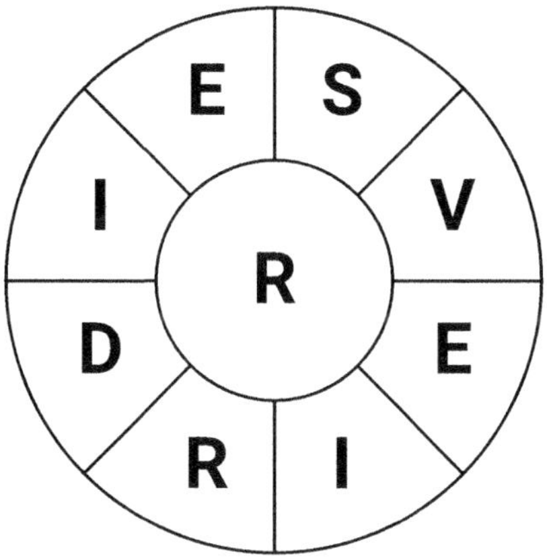


# PATHFINDER

**18**

Starting from the shaded letter, move up, down or sideways (but NOT diagonally) to find a route through the grid that spells out the 11 teams that have played in the ICC Women's Cricket World Cup since 2000. The route should form a continuous line through each of the letters in the grid, ending back at the shaded letter.

| R | I | H | B | A | I | W | A | I | A | T | S |
|---|---|---|---|---|---|---|---|---|---|---|---|
| E | L | S | A | N | L | E | S | D | N | K | I |
| N | A | E | D | G | A | R | T | N | I | A | P |
| D | I | L | A | L | S | T | I | N | A | L | D |
| S | R | A | N | E | U | A | S | D | E | A | N |
| A | K | N | A | T | H | E | E | I | Z | W | E |
| S | T | H | C | I | L | R | S | E | L | A | N |
| O | U | A | F | R | A | N | D | N | G | N | D |

## SCORECARD 19

Pakistan Women are batting first against Ireland Women in a fantasy WODI match at the National Stadium, Karachi. Can you crack the logical code behind the runs scored and work out how many runs Nida Dar and Iram Javed score?

| PAKISTAN Women | | |
|---|---|---|
| Sidra Amin | c Hunter b Kelly | 11 |
| Gull Feroza | lbw b Delany | 24 |
| Muneeba Ali (wk) | b J. Maguire | 13 |
| Omaima Sohail | run out | 0 |
| Aliyah Riaz | c Lewis b Canning | 54 |
| Nida Dar | lbw b Kelly | ? |
| Iram Javed | st Hunter b Canning | ? |

## MIDDLE ORDER 20

Arrange the letters found in **ALISON SIU** (HK) (*48 WT20I's, 2019-24*) in the grid below to form six five-letter words reading across and down.

**A L I S O N S I U**

| | R | W | C | |
|---|---|---|---|---|
| D | | | | S |
| O | | | | N |
| I | | | | E |
| | E | T | D | |

## FOURS 21

Can you identify the New Zealand women's cricketer (*30 WODI's, 2018-24*) whose surname can be placed after BEAR, STAND, CALM and TRACK to make two new words or phrases?

**BEAR**
**STAND**
**CALM**
**TRACK**

## MIXED UP PAIRS 22

Can you rearrange the pairs of letters to spell the name of a Pakistan women's cricketer *(21 WT20I's, 2017-24)*?

| AP | NA | IZ | LI | VA | ER | TA |
|---|---|---|---|---|---|---|

# PITCH IT UP



Enter the letters into their correct boxes in the vertical columns above to reveal the name of a women's international cricketer, their national team and four domestic teams they have played for around the cricket world.

|   |   |   |   |   |   |   |   |   |   |   |   |   |
|---|---|---|---|---|---|---|---|---|---|---|---|---|
|   |   |   |   |   | ■ |   |   |   |   |   |   | ■ |
|   |   |   |   |   |   |   |   |   | ■ | ■ | ■ | ■ |
|   |   | ■ |   |   |   |   |   |   |   |   | ■ | ■ |
|   |   |   |   |   |   |   |   | ■ |   |   |   | T |
|   |   |   |   |   |   |   |   |   |   | ■ | ■ | ■ |
|   |   |   |   |   |   | ■ |   |   |   |   |   | T |
| B | U | N | W | O | S | H | A | N | I | Z | A | ~~T~~ |
| G | O | S | E | B | A | L | I | P | D | R | S | ~~T~~ |
| Q | R | E | D | A | N | R | S | O | R | E | I |   |
| A | P | A | S | R | A | N | I | R | H | I |   |   |
| L | U | I | C | E | R | L | E | A | R |   |   |   |
| U | R |   | T | N |   |   | A |   |   |   |   |   |

# CRICKET (DING)BATS



Can you identify the cricket-related terms suggested by the images below?

**ANXIOUS T**

*tense T* SCARED T

*AGITATED T*

SKITTISH T ON EDGE T

APPREHENSIVE T

*worried t*

FRIGHTENED T

1. ..............................................

EXAM RESULTS

| | |
|---|---|
| MADDY | 85% |
| SUZIE | 81% |
| AMELIA | 78% |
| SOPHIE | 77% |
| FRAN | 75% |

2. ..............................................

# CRICKET CROSSWORD

## ACROSS

1. The batter at the bowling end (3-7)
8. City originally scheduled to host the final of the 2024 ICC Women's T20 World Cup (5)
9. and 7 down: Hampshire and England all-rounder (*34 WODI's, 2021-24*) (7)
10. The number of on-field umpires (3)
11. .......... Hartley, England left-arm spinner, now cricket commentator and podcaster (*28 WODI's, 2016-19*) (4)
12. Weather that typically causes a delay in match progress (4)
14. London .........., team that competes in The Hundred cricket tournament (6)
16. Divya .........., Canada all-rounder and current captain of national team (*12 WT20I's, 2021-23*) (6)
19. .......... leg, fielding position on leg side at around 45 degrees to the wicket (4)
20. and 21 across: Pakistan all-rounder and former captain (*160 WT20I's, 2010-24*) (4)
21. See 20 across (3)
23. Meg .........., Australia top-order batter and former captain (*103 WODI's, 2011-23*) (7)
24. Drop a catch (5)
25. New Zealand all-rounder and former captain, holds record for highest run scorer in WT20I's (*163 WODI's, 2006-24*) (5,5)

## DOWN

2. .......... Sparks, cricket team based in Dunedin, New Zealand and captained by 25 Across (5)
3. .......... Taylor, West Indies all-rounder and former captain (*160 WODI's, 2008-24*) (6)
4. .......... Slater, Yorkshire and Scotland medium-pace bowler (*23 WT20I's, 2022-24*) (6)
5. Yasmeen .........., Namibia middle-order batter and occassional wicket-keeper (*78 WT20I's, 2018-24*) (4)
6. Point in bowling action when the cricket ball leaves the bowler's hand (7)
7. See 9 Across (4)
8. Tour .........., schedule of cricket fixtures (5)
13. National cricket team captained by Winifred Duraisingam (8)
15. A player's or one team's turn to bat (7)
17. .......... Fahey, Australia off-spin bowler and member of World Cup winning team in 1997 (*40 WODI's, 1997-2001*) (5)
18. Scored when the batters run only once between the wickets (6)
19. .......... of wicket, the specific score at which a batter gets out (4)
21. A front foot shot played with a straight bat (5)
22. Aliya .........., Pakistan all-rounder (*99 WT20I's, 2014-24*) (4)

## VARIATION 26

Can you complete the grid so that every row and column contain each of the letters found in the surname of Jhulan **GOSWAMI** (IND) (*204 WODI's, 2002-22*)?

<table>
<tr><td></td><td>I</td><td></td><td></td><td></td><td></td><td></td></tr>
<tr><td></td><td></td><td>I</td><td></td><td>A</td><td></td><td>S</td></tr>
<tr><td></td><td></td><td></td><td></td><td></td><td></td><td></td></tr>
<tr><td></td><td>M</td><td></td><td>O</td><td></td><td>W</td><td></td></tr>
<tr><td>S</td><td></td><td></td><td></td><td>G</td><td></td><td>A</td></tr>
<tr><td></td><td>O</td><td></td><td></td><td></td><td>M</td><td></td></tr>
<tr><td>W</td><td></td><td></td><td></td><td>S</td><td></td><td></td></tr>
</table>

## MID-OFF 27

Can you identify the South Africa women's cricketer (*63 WT20I's, 2018-24*) whose surname fits in the sequence of words below?

**SIR**
**RIBS**
**?????**
**TRIBES**
**BLISTER**

## STAIRCASE 28

Arrange the surnames of the seven Australia women's cricketers listed below so that when placed in the horizontal rows of the grid, the letters of the diagonal 'staircase' spell out an eighth cricketer (AUS, *95 WT20I's, 2017-24*).

LUMSDEN GORDON BURNS HAGGETT HUNTER KENDALL PRICE

## ICC HALL OF FAME 29

Despite their names being scrambled can you identify the 13 women who have been inducted into the ICC Cricket Hall of Fame? The induction years are included as a guide.

2010 **CHARLEA OHYEEH TINFL** (ENG) ……………………

2011 **NAILBED RACKL** (AUS) ……………………

2012 **DINE WEAKBELL** (ENG) ……………………

2014 **EBBIED CHOYLEK** (NZ) ……………………

2015 **TYTEB NOWILS** (AUS) ……………………

2016 **RANKE NORTOL** (AUS) ……………………

2018 **LARICE RALTOY** (ENG) ……………………

2019 **NARTCHY TRACKZIPFIT** (AUS) ……………………

2020 **ISLA HARTSLAKE** (AUS) ……………………

2021 **ANJ RIBTINT** (ENG) ……………………

2022 **THECARLOT WADDERS** (ENG) ……………………

2023 **NAIAD ILJUDE** (IND) ……………………

2024 **TUNEE VIDDA** (IND) ……………………

## MISSING LETTERS 30

Working from letter to adjacent letter in any direction can you spell out the name of a Bangladesh women's cricketer (*88 WT20I's, 2013-24*)? You need to find the starting point and identify the missing letters.

| | | |
|---|---|---|
| ? | A | H |
| A | I | F |
| N | K | H |
| U | T | ? |

## HIT FOR SIX 31

Complete the grid so that every row and column, and every outlined area, contains each of the letters found in the surname of Laura **DELANY** (IRE) (*110 WT20I's, 2010-24*).

| | | | | | |
|---|---|---|---|---|---|
| Y | | | | | |
| | | | N | | |
| | | | | | |
| | A | | | | E |
| | | D | | L | |
| | | | | | |

# WORDSEARCH



The names of the 21 African countries or territories that are members of the International Cricket Council (ICC) have been hidden in the Wordsearch below. The names can be found written horizontally (forwards and backwards), vertically (up or down) or diagonally. Can you find them?

| | | | | | | | | | | | | | | | |
|---|---|---|---|---|---|---|---|---|---|---|---|---|---|---|---|
| E | B | I | S | O | U | N | E | L | R | K | E | M | A | Y | U |
| M | O | Z | A | M | B | I | Q | U | E | A | O | I | S | G | T |
| A | T | N | I | X | O | G | L | N | W | Z | B | L | A | M | S |
| G | S | U | R | M | H | E | Y | A | N | I | G | E | R | I | A |
| N | W | E | S | W | T | A | F | U | M | B | D | S | E | T | Z |
| O | A | D | L | B | O | T | S | A | O | C | Y | R | O | V | I |
| O | N | M | A | L | S | J | N | X | M | K | R | J | C | X | M |
| R | A | S | I | R | E | O | G | H | A | A | M | O | Y | S | B |
| E | V | A | T | W | L | H | A | Z | L | I | L | C | E | K | A |
| M | H | G | Q | A | Y | I | C | E | V | E | B | A | S | D | B |
| A | T | U | O | E | N | B | O | Y | S | N | H | M | W | R | W |
| C | N | G | S | A | I | N | T | H | E | L | E | N | A | I | E |
| F | H | A | Z | M | E | Z | I | M | B | S | Y | K | T | G | N |
| R | E | N | H | A | S | O | U | T | H | A | F | R | I | C | A |
| M | A | D | R | G | H | M | P | G | T | C | I | E | N | L | P |
| T | R | A | C | T | A | D | N | A | W | R | O | V | I | S | Y |

1. ..........
2. ..........
3. ..........
4. ..........
5. ..........
6. ..........
7. ..........
8. ..........
9. ..........
10. ..........
11. ..........
12. ..........
13. ..........
14. ..........
15. ..........
16. ..........
17. ..........
18. ..........
19. ..........
20. ..........
21. ..........

# CRICTETRIS



Drop each of the shapes from the top of the grid to spell the surnames of ten West Indies women's cricketers reading across. One of the shapes has been dropped to help you get started.

Note: The shapes should not be rotated or reflected and must be able to be dropped into the grid so that they come to rest on another shape or the grid bottom.

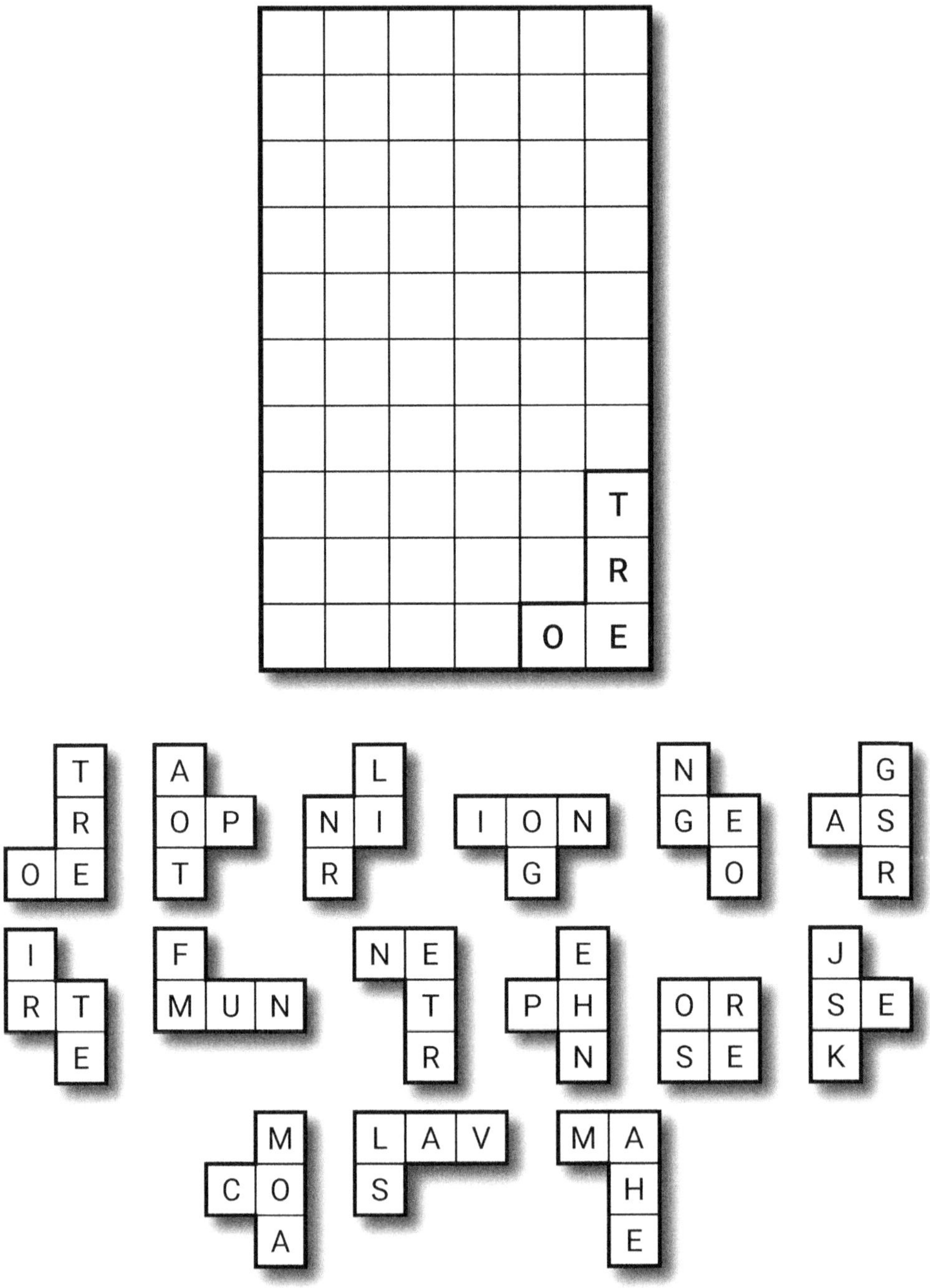

## TAILENDERS 34

The name of an England women's cricketer (*19 WT20I's, 2022-24*) can be inserted in the bottom row of the grid below to complete nine 3-letter words reading downwards. Can you identify them?

| E | W | T | B | S | A | H | G | L |
|---|---|---|---|---|---|---|---|---|
| L | A | O | U | E | S | U | E | I |
|  |  |  |  |  |  |  |  |  |

## INSIDE OUT 35

Enter a word in the spaces of each row to spell a seven letter word. When complete the shaded squares will spell out the surname of an Ireland women's cricketer (*50 WT20I's, 2019-24*).

| W | E | B |  |  |  | E |
|---|---|---|---|---|---|---|
| A | M |  |  |  | U | R |
| C | O | L |  |  |  | L |
| G |  |  |  | E | T | S |
| B | O |  |  |  | O | M |
| A | T | H |  |  |  | E |
| L |  |  |  | A | N | D |

## DIRECTION 36

Taking a letter from each segment of the circle in turn, can you spell out the name of a cricket ground and its location (8,8).

The ground hosted the final of the 2023 ICC Women's T20 World Cup. You need to find the starting points and identify the direction the names are spelt.

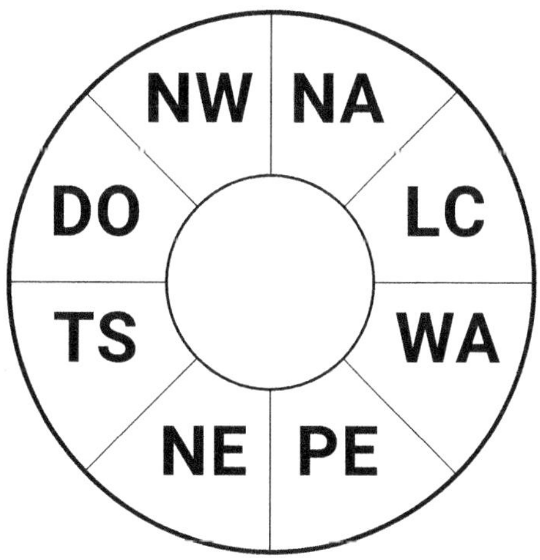


## CONUNDRUM 37

Can you unscramble the anagram to reveal the name of a New Zealand women's cricketer?

**MORE PILGRIMAGE** (NZ) (*36 WT20I's, 2022-24*)

## BUMP BALL 38

Can you identify the missing letters that complete the surnames of 6 Scotland women's cricketers?
Next, rearrange the missing letters to spell the surname of another Scotland women's cricketer (*38 WT20I's, 2021-24*).

| | | | | | |
|---|---|---|---|---|---|
| C | A | R | | E | R |
| S | P | | N | C | E |
| | A | I | N | E | Y |
| W | I | L | L | I | |
| S | | A | T | E | R |
| G | A | L | V | | N |

## FIVE DOWN 39

Insert letters into the grid below to form five words reading across. When complete, the name of an India women's cricketer (59 WT20I's, 2020-24) will be spelt out reading down the shaded squares.

| | | | | |
|---|---|---|---|---|
| F | | O | | S |
| N | | C | | E |
| S | | O | | P |
| W | | I | | K |
| B | | T | | E |

## SILHOUETTE 40

Can you name the women's international cricketer suggested by the images below?

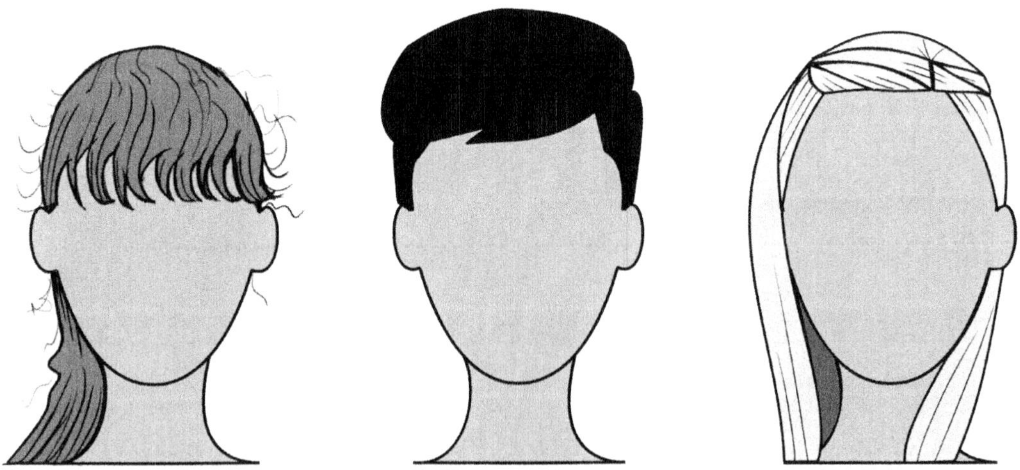

**SCOTLAND Women**
*58 WT20I's (2018-24)*

**INDIA Women**
*85 WT20I's (2019-24)*

**SOUTH AFRICA Women**
*154 WODI's (2007-22)*

# CRIDOKU 41

Fill in the squares of the grid so that each row, each column and each smaller 3x3 block contains all the letters which spell **NICKY SHAW** (ENG) (*70 WODI's, 1999-2010*) only once.

| | Y | A | K | | | | W | |
|---|---|---|---|---|---|---|---|---|
| H | | | | A | | N | | Y |
| | K | | | N | Y | | | A |
| | | C | | | | | | S |
| | W | K | | Y | | H | I | |
| S | | | | | | K | | |
| Y | | | A | H | | | S | |
| C | | H | | W | | | | K |
| | S | | | | N | A | H | |

# DO YOU KNOW? 42

The first ever Cricket World Cup was contested by women in 1973 - two years before the first Men's World Cup. Do you know which team won the trophy?

A. Australia
B. England
C. India
D. New Zealand
E. West Indies

# CRICKET CIRCLES 43

Replace the question marks with letters so that the letters in each circle can be arranged to spell the surnames of three women's cricketers who all play for the same national team. Can you name the cricketers and the team?

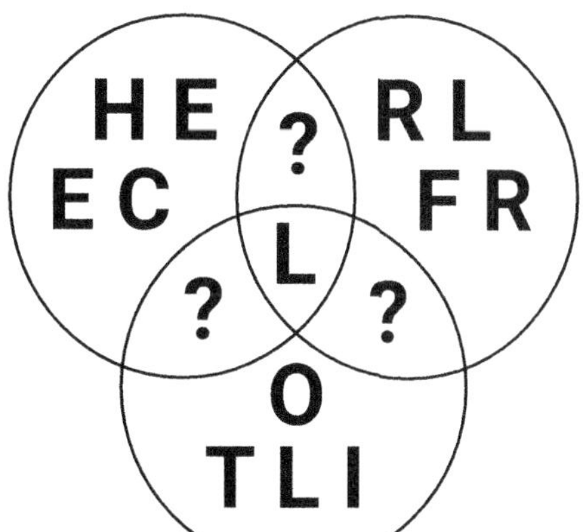

# FOLLOW ON



Every answer to each clue (except the first) starts with the last letter of the preceding answer, and when entered into the grid follows a spiral path reading anti-clockwise to the centre. When complete, the shaded diagonal squares will spell out the name of a women's international cricketer and a domestic team they have played for.

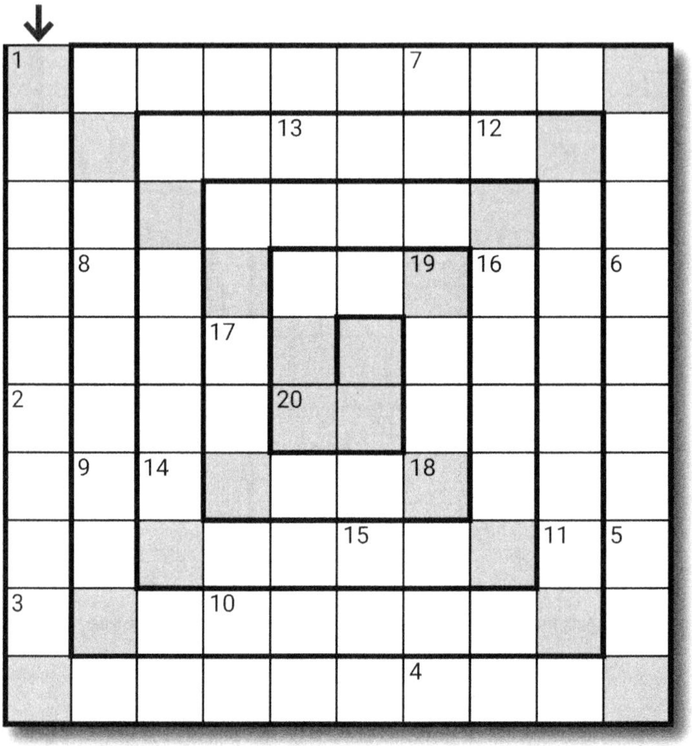


1. Bring a task or activity to an end (6)
2. A person admired for bravery, achievements or qualities (4)
3. Kept busy and active (8)
4. A period of ten years (6)
5. Supply with necessary items for a particular purpose (5)
6. Light-hearted; funny and not serious (7)
7. Make or enact laws (9)
8. Very impressive; grand in scale or character (4)
9. The person in charge of a meeting (5)
10. Consider something again, especially to change it for the better (7)
11. Input device for putting information into a computer (8)
12. To attract attention or interest (4)
13. A woman who serves customers in a cafe or restaurant (8)
14. Inhale audibly through the nose to detect a smell (5)
15. Easily broken or damaged (7)
16. Feeling or sense of extreme happiness or excitement (8)
17. Performers in theatre productions or in films, TV, etc (6)
18. Deliberately insult someone by ignoring (4)
19. To hold resposible for a failure or wrong (5)
20. Organ of hearing and balance (3)

# CROSSWORD 4s

## 45

Can you complete the puzzle by correctly placing the four-letter cricket-related words into the crossword?

STEP NETS TOUR PULL NEXT CLUB LINE SHOT NICK DEEP
OVAL BALL PATH WAIT BYES REST PADS SAVE BEAT SLIP

# BOX CLEVER

## 46

Can you shade-in some of the boxes in the grid below to reveal something connected with Mithali Raj (IND) (*232 WODI's, 1999-2022*)? First, fully shade-in all the boxes containing the letter **A**. Then, shade-in all the boxes that contain one other letter found in **MITHALI RAJ** to spell out the answer in the grid.

Tip: Use a pencil to fully shade-in the relevant boxes.

| I | H | T | J | T | I | L | A | ■ | R | H | T | J | I | L | H | I | L | J |
|---|---|---|---|---|---|---|---|---|---|---|---|---|---|---|---|---|---|---|
| L | ■ | A | R | I | J | T | R | H | ■ | J | I | L | H | I | ■ | R | ■ | H |
| T | J | H | ■ | H | L | I | ■ | A | R | T | A | R | ■ | J | A | T | I | L |
| H | I | R | L | T | J | H | R | J | A | L | ■ | I | A | T | R | A | ■ | J |
| L | A | H | I | R | ■ | L | A | R | ■ | T | R | A | ■ | J | I | L | R | T |
| T | ■ | J | T | H | A | T | H | I | L | H | J | T | J | L | ■ | R | A | I |

## ODD ONE OUT

**47**

Can you identify which one of the following facts is NOT true about Australia women's cricketer Ellyse Perry?

**ELLYSE PERRY**
**AUSTRALIA WOMEN**
*147 WODI's: 3,958 runs, 165 wickets*

A. Ellyse made her international debut in June 2007 at the age of 16 years and 8 months, becoming the youngest-ever cricketer to represent Australia.

B. A month after making her international cricket debut Ellyse played her first match for the Australia women's football team, scoring a goal within two minutes.

C. Despite her status as one of the greatest-ever women's cricketers, Ellyse has only captained her national team on just two occassions - both WT20I's against New Zealand.

D. Ellyse has been the recipient of numerous awards, including the ICC Women's Cricketer of the Decade for 2011-2020.

---

## PARTNERSHIP

**48**

For each of the word pairs listed, identify the 4-letter word (and surname of a women's international cricketer) that can be placed after the first word and before the second word to make two new words or phrases. Enter your answers in the grid and rearrange the shaded letters to reveal the name of an ICC Associate member.

| | | | | | | | |
|---|---|---|---|---|---|---|---|
| CAR ............ POT | | (shaded) | | | SCO (*2018-24*) |
| FENCE ............ BOX | | | (shaded) | | NED (*2018-22*) |
| BIRD ............ TUB | (shaded) | | | | AUS (*1957-58*) |
| FRONT ............ NUMBER | | | | (shaded) | NZ (*1973*) |
| UP ............ TOP | | (shaded) | | | HK (*2019-24*) |
| BUS ............ WELL | | | (shaded) | | VAN (*2019-24*) |

Name of ICC member: ..................................................

## SIXERS 49

The arrows in this grid indicate that the number on the next ball is lower. Can you complete the grid so that all rows and columns contain the numbers 1 to 6?

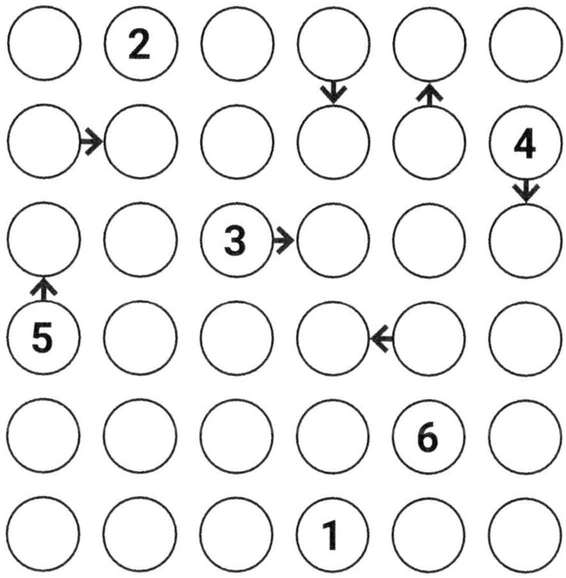


## INSIDE OUT 50

Enter a word in the spaces of each row to spell a seven letter word. When complete the shaded squares will spell out the surname of a Hong Kong women's cricketer (*54 WT20I's, 2019-24*).

| | | | | | | |
|---|---|---|---|---|---|---|
| P | | | | O | C | K |
| C | A | | | | E | L |
| W | | | | T | L | E |
| S | T | E | | | | D |
| C | | | | M | I | C |
| P | E | A | | | | S |
| S | A | | | | N | T |

## ROTATION 51

Find the starting point and fill in the blanks to reveal the name (7,9) of a Sri Lanka women's cricketer (*13 WT20I's, 2022-24*). Only alternate letters are shown.

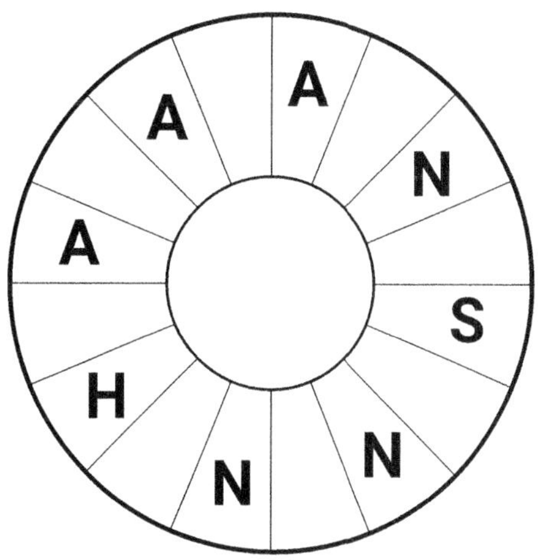

# 15 QUESTIONS WORDSEARCH



Can you find the answers to these quiz questions about women's international cricket hidden in the Wordsearch below? The answers can be found written across (forwards and backwards), up or down or diagonally?

| | | | | | | | | | | | | | | | |
|---|---|---|---|---|---|---|---|---|---|---|---|---|---|---|---|
| C | R | O | D | N | I | M | I | B | A | F | E | L | R | S | H |
| F | A | T | I | C | Z | A | Q | R | E | N | P | T | I | Y | A |
| X | I | S | M | A | H | I | K | A | G | A | U | R | W | O | I |
| B | D | L | D | S | K | A | P | Z | N | M | D | H | X | D | N |
| S | N | O | T | T | O | C | M | I | K | B | I | C | B | R | G |
| A | I | F | B | U | V | U | H | L | A | T | Q | R | M | H | M |
| E | O | V | A | L | G | A | T | N | E | S | V | U | A | I | D |
| R | G | X | N | I | M | V | O | H | B | R | I | H | N | U | W |
| D | N | A | G | E | H | I | E | S | A | N | G | C | B | O | A |
| E | W | E | L | I | P | A | Z | L | D | F | I | T | G | E | L |
| R | P | F | A | L | T | G | P | I | Y | C | R | S | C | U | A |
| T | N | H | D | H | I | C | A | E | N | S | A | I | E | Y | M |
| I | T | Z | E | N | U | V | X | L | A | L | F | R | C | J | K |
| U | K | R | S | A | D | O | E | N | G | R | P | H | I | A | T |
| S | E | I | H | T | I | M | S | H | E | O | L | C | L | D | F |
| C | W | M | U | L | H | P | E | R | T | S | U | S | O | T | E |

1. In which city was the first-ever final of the Women's Cricket World Cup held?
2. 'The Victoria ..........,' nickname of the Uganda Women's national cricket team?
3. By what name is Malahide Cricket Club Ground, Ireland women's largest cricket venue, also known?
4. Jannillea .........., West Indies women's cricketer who has the same surname as Scotland's most populous city?
5. What is the surname of sisters Sharon and Janette, who played international cricket for Australia Women, the former playing in the 1973, 1978, 1982 and 1988 World Cups?
6. Which women's national cricket team is captained by Roberta Moretti Avery?
7. What animal features on the logo/badge of the Netherlands women's cricket team?
8. Which current England women's cricketer has also played international cricket for UAE?
9. What is the nickname of South Africa women's cricketer Mignon du Preez?
10. Which ICC Full member's first appearance at a Women's Cricket World Cup was in 2022?
11. What country is scheduled to host the ICC Women's Cricket World Cup in 2025?
12. In April 2023, who became the first female on-field umpire to officiate in a men's international between two Full member nations?
13. Karen .........., captain of England's winning team in 1993 ICC Women's Cricket World Cup?
14. What was the name of the world's first women's cricket club, established in Yorkshire in 1887?
15. In addition to New Zealand, for which other nation has Bernadine Bezuidenhout also played international cricket?

## MISSING LETTERS 53

Working from letter to adjacent letter in any direction can you spell out the name of a Scotland women's cricketer (*49 WT20I's, 2018-24*)?
You need to find the starting point and identify the missing letters.

| | | |
|---|---|---|
| ? | B | ? |
| Y | C | R |
| R | A | Y |
| ? | T | ? |

## MIDDLE ORDER 54

Arrange the letters found in **SIDRA AMIN** (PAK) (*69 WODI's, 2011-24*) in the grid below to form six five-letter words reading across and down.

**SIDRA AMIN**

| | | | | |
|---|---|---|---|---|
| ■ | A | P | G | ■ |
| S | | | | T |
| F | | | | L |
| A | | | | E |
| ■ | S | C | E | ■ |

## ICC MEMBERS 55

The solutions to these seven clues are all ICC member countries and incorporate the letters found in the names of the women's international cricketers listed below. Each answer involves the addition of extra letters to name the ICC member. When complete, place one of the additional letters in the shaded box to reveal the name of another ICC member country.

MALI SANA TARI ~~READ~~ WANI ARAA RANI

Capital city and ICC Region:

| Clue | | | | | | | | | | Shaded |
|---|---|---|---|---|---|---|---|---|---|---|
| 1. Dublin, Europe | | R | E | | A | | D | | | |
| 2. San Jose, Americas | | | | | | | | | | |
| 3. Bucharest, Europe | | | | | | | | | | |
| 4. Canberra, East-Asia Pacific | | | | | | | | | | |
| 5. Gaborone, Africa | | | | | | | | | | |
| 6. Mbabane, Africa | | | | | | | | | | |
| 7. Kuala Lumpur, Asia | | | | | | | | | | |

Name of ICC member: ........................................................................

## RUNS TEASER 56

USA Women have just completed batting in a WT20I match. Can you work out how many runs Gargi Bhogle, Aditiba Chudasama, Disha Dhingra, Anika Kolan and Sindhu Sriharsha each scored if:

| | |
|---|---|
| BHOGLE + SRIHARSHA = | 38 runs |
| CHUDASAMA + KOLAN = | 62 runs |
| SRIHARSHA + DHINGRA = | 27 runs |
| BHOGLE + CHUDASAMA = | 49 runs |
| DHINGRA + BHOGLE = | 53 runs |

**Runs scored:**

| Gargi | Aditiba | Disha | Anika | Sindhu |
|---|---|---|---|---|
| BHOGLE ......... | CHUDASAMA ......... | DHINGRA ......... | KOLAN ......... | SRIHARSHA ......... |

## VARIATION 57

Can you complete the grid so that every row and column contain each of the letters found in the surname of Sunette **LOUBSER** (SA) (*60 WODI's, 2007-14*)?

| | | | | | | |
|---|---|---|---|---|---|---|
| U | | | S | | E | |
| | | R | | | | B |
| | | | | O | | |
| L | | | | | S | |
| | | O | | B | | E |
| S | R | | | | U | |
| | | L | | | | |

## SIX DOWN 58

Insert letters into the grid below to form six words reading across. When complete, the name of a West Indies women's cricketer (*9 WTests, 1976-79*) will be spelt out reading down the shaded squares.

| | | | | |
|---|---|---|---|---|
| G | | O | | E |
| B | | A | | D |
| T | | T | | R |
| V | | E | | S |
| A | | A | | A |
| R | | B | | L |

## CONUNDRUM 59

Can you unscramble the anagram to reveal the name of an Ireland women's cricketer?

**CALM CAFETERIA** (IRE) (*53 WODI's, 1999-2017*)

# SQUARE CUT 60

Can you transfer the squares into the blank grid below so that a two-letter word is formed by each pair of adjoining letters and the name (6,6) of an India women's cricketer (*89 WODI's, 2014-24*) is spelt out reading clockwise around the outside perimeter.

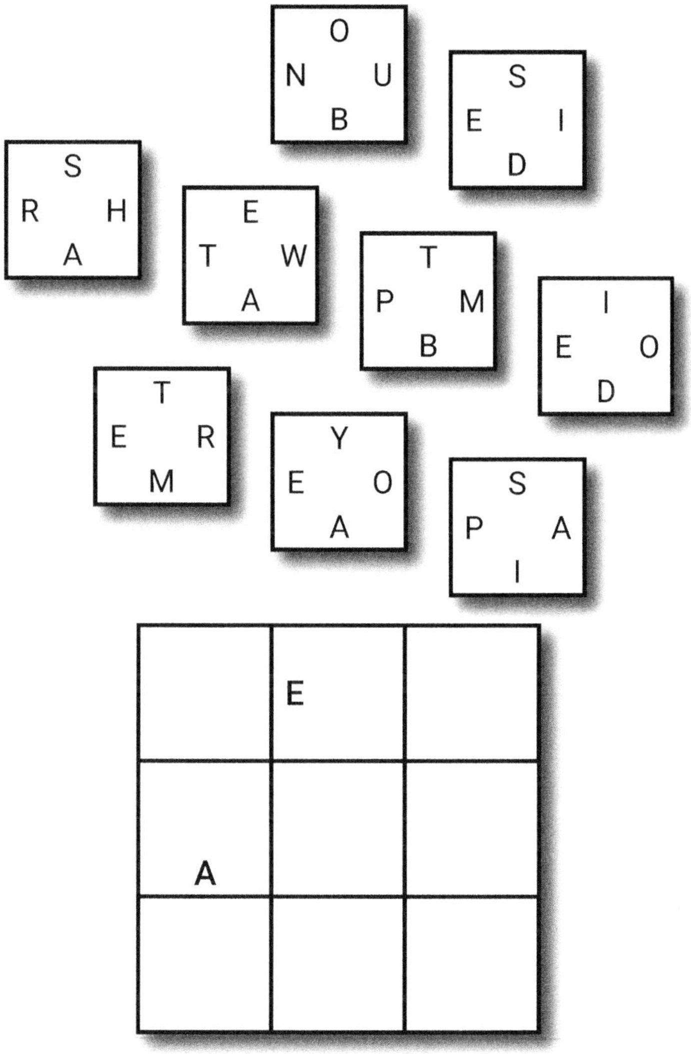


# MIXED UP THREE'S 61

Can you rearrange the groups of letters to spell the name of an international women's cricketer *(118 WODI's, 2003-19)*?

| ARD | SHA | RIW | KAL | SHI | ENE | ASI |
|---|---|---|---|---|---|---|

# WHO PLAYS WHO?



It's the Quarter-finals of the ICC Cricket World Cup. From the information below can you work out who plays who?

"WE PLAY A TEAM WITH A LETTER **T** IN ITS NAME."

**SOUTH AFRICA**

"OUR OPPONENT HAS A LETTER **L** IN ITS NAME."

**NEW ZEALAND**

"OUR OPPONENT HAS A LETTER **D** IN ITS NAME."

**WEST INDIES**

"WE PLAY A TEAM WITH A LETTER **I** IN ITS NAME."

**INDIA**

"WE PLAY A TEAM WITH A LETTER **S** IN ITS NAME."

**SRI LANKA**

"OUR OPPONENT HAS A LETTER **U** IN ITS NAME."

**PAKISTAN**

"OUR OPPONENT HAS A LETTER **E** IN ITS NAME."

**ENGLAND**

"WE PLAY A TEAM WITH A LETTER **R** IN ITS NAME."

**AUSTRALIA**

| QUARTER FINALS |
|---|
| v |
| v |
| v |
| v |

## NAME BOGGLER 63

The surnames of ten cricketers who have featured in limited overs matches for Australia Women since 2000 are hidden in the grid below. How many surnames can you find?
Each name can only be spelt by moving from letter to adjacent letter, including diagonally. No individual letter can be used more than once in each name. Players sharing the same name only count as one.

**Target:**
6 cricketers = GOOD, 8 cricketers = EXCELLENT, 10 cricketers = OUTSTANDING

| | | | |
|---|---|---|---|
| O | T | A | W |
| N | R | H | L |
| G | A | E | S |
| C | M | Y | N |

## MISSING VOWELS 64

Despite all the vowels being removed can you identify the following cricket-related terms? Note: To complicate matters the gaps between the words have been rearranged.

1. BTN DP DCT CH ..................
2. HT THB LLT WC ..................
3. NCM NGB TTR ..................
4. TNW CK THL ..................
5. BW LDT HRG HT HGT ..................
6. HL DP NND ..................
7. NPL YB LDL VRY ..................
8. FR MTH ST RK ..................
9. BTT NGF RD RW ..................
10. CCP YNGT HC RS ..................

## OUTSIDE EDGE 65

Can you divide the following words into two and transfer the letters into the grid below to spell the surnames of 10 women's international cricketers? Note, the divided letters can be placed either at the start or end of the cricketer's name.

| ~~WEEDY~~ | LAUGH | MAST | SALONS | TRAM |
|---|---|---|---|---|
| STAKE | SHIN | FATHER | TELL | GENTS |

LIST OF CRICKETERS

| | | | |
|---|---|---|---|
| WEE | **RAKKO** | DY | SL, *89 WODI's, 2006-18* |
| | **AR** | | IRE, *9 WT20I's, 2023-24* |
| | **IOT** | | AUS, *22 WODI's, 2005-10* |
| | **OM** | | NED, *51 WODI's, 1995-2011* |
| | **MPLO** | | HK, *26 WT20I's, 2019-24* |
| | **HO** | | PNG, *23 WT20I's, 2019-24* |
| | **HUR** | | SA, *8 WODI's, 1997-99* |
| | **ARM** | | BAN, *16 WT20I's, 2013-19* |
| | **ALHO** | | IND, *41 WODI's, 2003-13* |
| | **IRWEA** | | WI, *10 Tests, 1976-79* |

## CRICKET UMPIRES 66

Can you match the female cricket umpires to the correct nationality?

| | |
|---|---|
| Kim Cotton | England |
| Mary Waldron | South Africa |
| Saleema Imtiaz | New Zealand |
| Anna Harris | Pakistan |
| Claire Polosak | Ireland |
| Shivam Mishra | Australia |
| Lauren Agenbag | India |

## CONNECTION? 67

The women's international cricketers listed below have something unusual in common. Can you spot what it is?

GEORGIA GUY (NZ)
LOUISE MCCARTHY (IRE)
MELISSA BULOW (AUS)
UDENI DONA (UAE)
SOPHIA DUNKLEY (ENG)

# CRICKET JUMBO CODEWORD



Each number in the grid represents a different letter of the alphabet. Can you complete the grid correctly and also identify the surnames of 10 Australia women's cricketers hidden in the squares?

| | | | | | | | | | | | | |
|---|---|---|---|---|---|---|---|---|---|---|---|---|
| 2 | 12 | 23 | 17 | 23 | 19 | 11 | | 26 | 2 | 23 | 23 | 19 |
| | 11 | | 9 | | 10 | | 26 | | 9 | | 17 | |
| 26 | 23 | 21 | 12 | 25 | 11 | | 1 | 21 | 10 | 7 | 11 | 12 |
| | 12 | | 10 | | 11 | | 12 | | | | 12 | |
| 9 | 3 | 13 | 15 | 7 | | 16 | 21 | 15 | 2 | 2 | 11 | 3 |
| | 11 | | 26 | | 8 | | 18 | | 12 | | 22 | |
| 23 | 12 | 25 | 1 | 9 | 12 | 3 | | 19 | 15 | 10 | 22 | |
| | | | 11 | | 11 | | 9 | | 25 | | | |
| 1 | 11 | 9 | 3 | 5 | 11 | 9 | 12 | | 11 | 9 | 26 | 14 |
| | 22 | | | | 20 | | 25 | | | | 11 | |
| 20 | 23 | 23 | 13 | | 11 | 24 | 1 | 15 | 18 | 15 | 7 | 26 |
| | | | 9 | | 12 | | 9 | | 4 | | | |
| | 22 | 21 | 26 | 7 | | 22 | 15 | 12 | 9 | 8 | 8 | 11 |
| | 4 | | 23 | | 1 | | 25 | | 13 | | 11 | |
| 12 | 9 | 15 | 10 | 18 | 23 | 5 | | 6 | 11 | 4 | 4 | 14 |
| | 25 | | | | 15 | | 2 | | 4 | | 4 | |
| 8 | 15 | 11 | 4 | 3 | 26 | | 15 | 25 | 11 | 18 | 23 | 24 |
| | 9 | | 15 | | 7 | | 19 | | 26 | | 5 | |
| 18 | 4 | 9 | 3 | 11 | | 2 | 11 | 12 | 26 | 15 | 26 | 7 |

A B C D E F G H I J K L M N O P Q R S T U V W X Y Z

| 1 | 2 | 3 | 4 | 5 | 6 | 7 | 8 | 9 | 10 | 11 | 12 | 13 |
|---|---|---|---|---|---|---|---|---|---|---|---|---|
| | | | | W | | | | | | | | |
| **14** | **15** | **16** | **17** | **18** | **19** | **20** | **21** | **22** | **23** | **24** | **25** | **26** |
| | | | | | | | U | | | | | |

## STAIRCASE 69

Arrange the surnames of the seven England women's cricketers listed below so that when placed in the horizontal rows of the grid, the letters of the diagonal 'staircase' spell out an eighth cricketer (ENG, *28 WODI's, 2016-19*).

PLIMMER BIRCH HOLDEN GOATMAN WILKS GRUNDY DANIELS

## BUMP BALL 70

Can you identify the missing letters that complete the surnames of 6 New Zealand women's cricketers?
Next, rearrange the missing letters to spell the surname of another New Zealand women's cricketer (*66 WODI's, 1999-2008*).

| | | | | | |
|---|---|---|---|---|---|
| J | E | | S | E | N |
| B | R | O | | N | E |
| | U | R | N | E | R |
| M | A | C | K | | Y |
| C | U | R | T | I | |
| D | | O | L | A | N |

## HIT FOR SIX 71

Complete the grid so that every row and column, and every outlined area, contains each of the letters found in the surname of Irene **VAN ZYL** (NAM) (*64 WT20I's, 2019-24*).

| | | | | | |
|---|---|---|---|---|---|
| | | | | | L |
| | Y | | | | |
| | | | N | | |
| | | | | | V |
| A | | | | | |
| | | Z | | | |

# CRICKET CROSSWORD

**ACROSS**

4. .......... Road, cricket ground in Leicester, England that regularly hosts women's international cricket matches (5)
7. Alyssa .........., Australia wicket-keeper batter and current captain (*162 WT20I's, 2010-24*) (6)
10. India opening batter, played in 2017 ICC Cricket World Cup (*73 WODI's,2009-21*) (5,4)
11. The second of two intervals during a full day's play (3)
12. Beth .........., Australia top-order batter (*106 WT20I's, 2016-24*) (6)
13. Raised stitching around the circumference of a cricket ball (4)
16. Material used for stitching at 13 across (6)
17. 30 yard feature that impacts fielding positions in limited overs cricket (6)
20. .......... Sobhana, RCB and India all-rounder (*6 WT20I's, 2024*) (4)
22. Shakera .........., West Indies medium-pace bowler (*100 WODI's, 2008-22*) (6)
24. .......... practice, used for developing batting and bowling technique (3)
26. ICC Associate member, located in the Irish Sea (4,2,3)
27. .......... Tucker, Western Province and South Africa all-rounder (*14 WT20I's, 2022-23*) (5)
28. Danni .......... - Hodge, England top-order batter (*164 WT20I's, 2010-24*) (5)

**DOWN**

1. see 5 down (4)
2. Pakistan all-rounder and former captain, now TV & radio commentator (*120 WODI's, 2005-19*) (4,3)
3. Cricket team that competes in Ireland's Women's Super Series, captained by Rebecca Stokell (7)
5. and 1 down: Unorthodox batting stroke also known as the paddle scoop (4)
6. Run .........., task of team batting last (5)
8. .......... arm, an illegal method of bowling (5)
9. Method of dismissal in which the wicket-keeper breaks the batter's wicket (7)
14. .......... Iqbal, Pakistan medium-pace bowler, in 2012 became the first player to take a hat-trick in WT20I's (*92 WODI's, 2005-17*) (7)
15. Northern .........., former women's cricket team that represented Yorkshire and North East England (8)
18. Shamilia .........., Barbados and West Indies pace bowler (*77 WT20I's, 2014-24*) (7)
19. Shafali .........., India top-order batter (*85` WT20I's, 2019-24*) (5)
21. .......... Colvin, England left-arm spinner (*72 WODI's, 2006-13*) (5)
23. During play, a cricket ball that cannot be found or recovered (4)
25. The lower-order of a batting line-up (4)

## SIDE ON

73

Can you pair the following words and transfer them into the list below to spell the names of 10 women's international cricketers?

FOOT MAIL SO MESH FAR NEW ERA
RAM FOLD CAMP LOVE HAIL PEN
CAR RANT BROAD PER ROLL IS BELLE

| | |
|---|---|
| Shemaine ........................ | WI, *114 WODI's, 2009-24* |
| Hasini ........................ | SL, *84 WT20I's 2014-24* |
| Mona ........................ | IND, *26 WODI's, 2012-19* |
| Shabnim ........................ | SA, *127 WODI's, 2007-22* |
| Jean ........................ | IRE, *8 WODI's, 2007-09* |
| Louise ........................ | AUS, *10 WODI's, 2000-05* |
| Natasha ........................ | ENG, *18 WT20I's, 2013-21* |
| Denise ........................ | SCO, *3 WODI's, 2001* |
| Omaima ........................ | PAK, *55 WT20Is, 2018-24* |
| Molly ........................ | NZ, *11 WODI's, 2021-24* |

---

## CRICKET (DING)BATS

74

Can you identify the cricket-related terms suggested by the images below?

**GOOD** (SA)
**MARSH** (ENG)
**H** (AUS)
**MCC** (IRE)

1. ........................

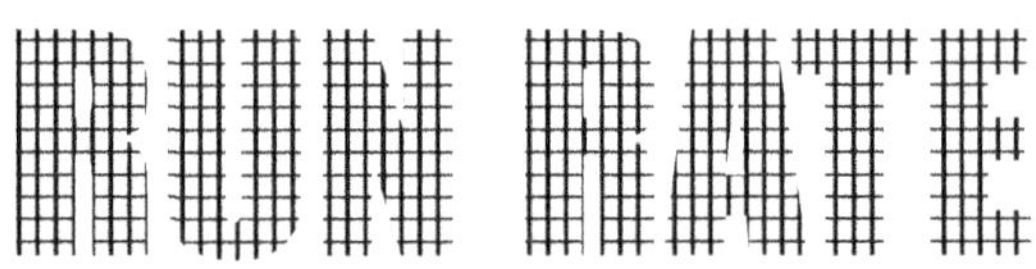


2. ........................

# CONUNDRUM 75

Can you unscramble the anagram to reveal the name of a Pakistan women's cricketer?

**SAUNA BATHS** (PAK) *(35 WT20I's, 2022-24)*

# RECORD HOLDER 76

Sally Barton is the oldest international cricketer of all time - both male or female.

Sally set the record on 16 June 2024 playing for Gibraltar Women against Croatia Women in the Women's Central Europe Cup held in the Czech Republic. How old was Sally?

A. 55 years, 149 days
B. 61 years, 293 days
C. 67 years, 24 days
D. 73 years, 139 days

# BATTING ORDER 77

Can you rearrange the boxes of the grid below to spell the name of a women's international cricketer *(109 WODI's, 1993-2007)*?

| | | |
|---|---|---|
| NF | CK | TH |
| AT | RY | IT |
| CA | ZP | RI |

# PATHFINDER 78

Starting from the shaded letter, move up, down or sideways (but NOT diagonally) to find the route through the grid that spells out 10 cricket fielding positions. The route should form a continuous loop through each of the letters in the grid, ending back at the shaded square.

| | | | | | | | | | | | |
|---|---|---|---|---|---|---|---|---|---|---|---|
| E | P | E | M | G | E | N | I | F | G | E | L |
| R | S | E | I | D | L | E | O | N | L | R | E |
| L | I | K | T | W | I | C | G | N | O | A | U |
| L | Y | M | E | K | C | K | E | S | L | I | Q |
| O | D | I | D | E | I | W | T | Y | L | P | S |
| F | F | A | N | E | A | R | N | T | F | R | E |
| H | T | M | B | P | W | D | I | E | R | A | V |
| I | R | D | A | C | K | P | O | X | T | C | O |

# CROSS OVER

79

The answers in this puzzle are the 51 women's international cricketers who have taken the most number of WT20I wickets. Can you complete the puzzle?

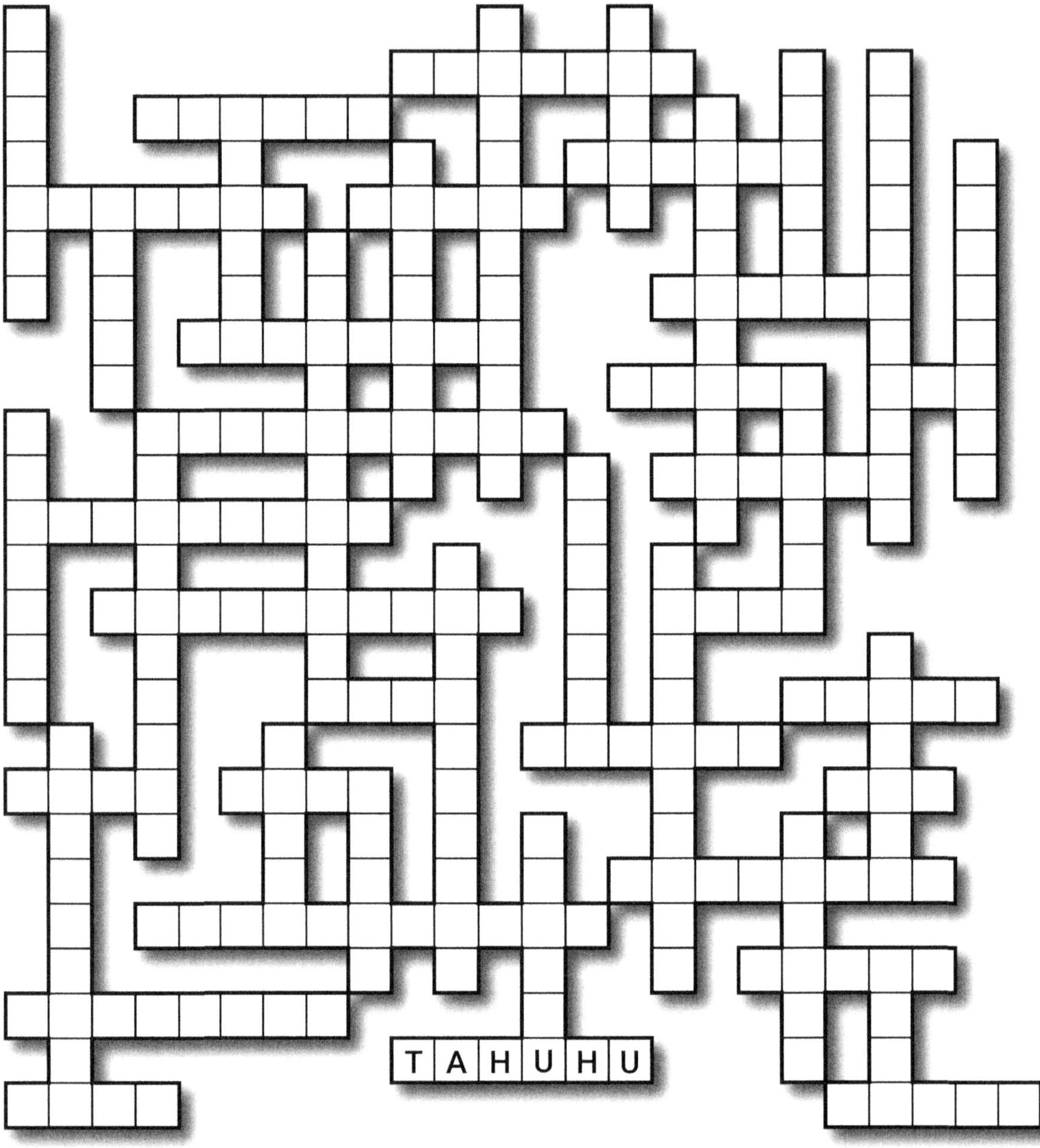


*3 LETTERS*
NIDA **DAR** (PAK) *144*
SANA **MIR** (PAK) *89*

*4 LETTERS*
**ABEL** Queentor (KEN) *80*
**CHAN** Betty (HK) *79*
**CHAN** Kary (HK) *82*
**GUNN** Jenny (HK) *75*
**KAPP** Marizanne (SA) *88*
**KERR** Amelia (NZ) *93*

*5 LETTERS*
Rumana **AHMED** (BAN) *75*
Nahida **AKTER** (BAN) *103*
**AWEKO** Concy (UGA) *109*
**DALEY** Shanel (WI) *72*
**GLENN** Sarah (ENG) *84*
**GREEN** Kayleen (NAM) *69*
**PERRY** Ellyse (AUS) *126*
**YADAV** Poonam (IND) *98*
**YADAV** Radha (IND) *91*

*6 LETTERS*
**DELANY** Laura (IRE) *85*
**DEVINE** Sophie (NZ) *117*
**DOTTIN** Deandra (WI) *67*
**HAZELL** Danni (ENG) *85*
**ISMAIL** Shabnim (SA) *123*
SALMA **KHATUN** (BAN) *84*

**MAHESH** Vaishnave (UAE) *90*
Nashra **SANDHU** (PAK) *65*
**SCHUTT** Megan (AUS) *145*
**SHARMA** Deepti (IND) *135*
~~**TAHUHU** Lea (NZ) *93*~~
**TAYLOR** Stafanie (WI) *98*

*7 LETTERS*
**GARDNER** Ashleigh (AUS) *78*
**ISHIMWE** Henriette (RWA) *109*
**KAMUNYA** Perice (TAN) *67*
**MBABAZI** Janet (UGA) *80*
**WACHIRA** Esther (KEN) *66*

*8 LETTERS*
**FLETCHER** Afy (WI) *83*
**JONASSEN** Jess (AUS) *96*
**KASPEREK** Leigh (NZ) *81*
**MATTHEWS** Hayley (WI) *103*
**MOHAMMED** Anisa (WI) *125*

*9 LETTERS*
**RANAWEERA** Inoko (SL) *92*
**SHRUBSOLE** Anya (ENG) *102*

*10 LETTERS*
**BOOCHATHAM** Nattaya (THA) *119*
**ECCLESTONE** Sophie (ENG) *131*
**KAMCHOMPHU** Onnicha (THA) *79*
**PRABODHANI** Udeshika (SL) *84*
**PUTTHAWONG** Thipatcha (THA) *70*
**VAN NIEKERK** Dane (SA) *65*

*11 LETTERS*
**SCIVER-BRUNT** Katherine (ENG) *114*
**SCIVER-BRUNT** Nat (ENG) *89*
**SIRIWARDENE** Shashikala (SL) *77*
**SUTTHIRUANG** Chanida (THA) *75*

## STEPLADDER 80

Climb from **LEAH** at the bottom of the ladder to **PAUL** at the top by changing just one letter to form a word and without disturbing the order of the remaining letters. The clues are provided to help you out but are not in the correct order.

LEAH PAUL plays for Ireland Women (*35 WODI's, 2017-24*).

| Clue | Ladder |
|---|---|
| | PAUL |
| Main role in a film or play | |
| Reach the ground after jumping | |
| Container with a curved handle | |
| Give temporary use of something | |
| Placed or put down on a surface | |
| Settled a debt | |
| | LEAH |

## PAIR UP 81

The 4-letter surnames of seven England women's cricketers are jumbled up in the grid below. Can you match the two pair of letters and work out which is not used?

| | | | | |
|---|---|---|---|---|
| AN | WE | LA | BE | NG |
| WO | IT | NO | GU | SM |
| HA | LL | DE | MB | RO |

# CRIDOKU 82

Fill in the squares of the grid so that each row, each column and each smaller 3x3 block contains all the letters which spell **GWEN SMITH** (WI) (*4 WODI's, 1997*) only once.

| | | | | | | | | |
|---|---|---|---|---|---|---|---|---|
| T | | W | E | | | | | M |
| | E | | | | W | | I | |
| | | | | I | N | | | H |
| | N | E | | | | | | W |
| | | H | | | | T | | |
| G | | | | | | M | N | |
| I | | | H | M | | | | |
| | M | | S | | | | H | |
| E | | | | | T | I | | G |

# CRICKET CIRCLES 83

Replace the question marks with letters so that the letters in each circle can be arranged to spell the surnames of three women's cricketers who all play for the same national team. Can you name the cricketers and the team?

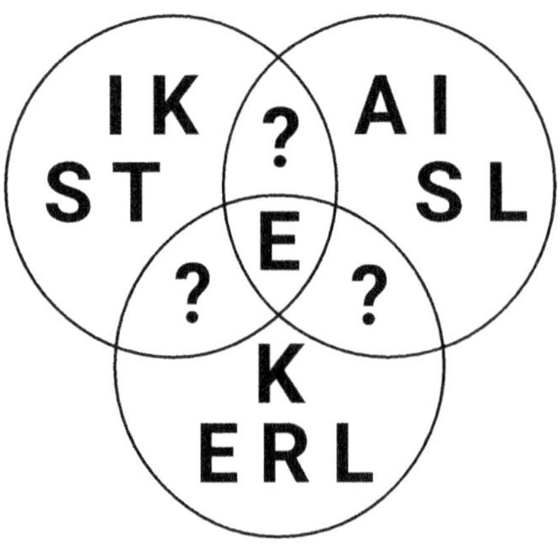


# MID-OFF 84

Can you identify the England women's cricketer (*10 WODI's, 2023-24*) whose surname fits in the sequence of words below?

**ELF**
**LIFE**
**?????**
**RELIEF**
**FERTILE**

# SILHOUETTE 85

Can you name the women's international cricketer suggested by the images below?

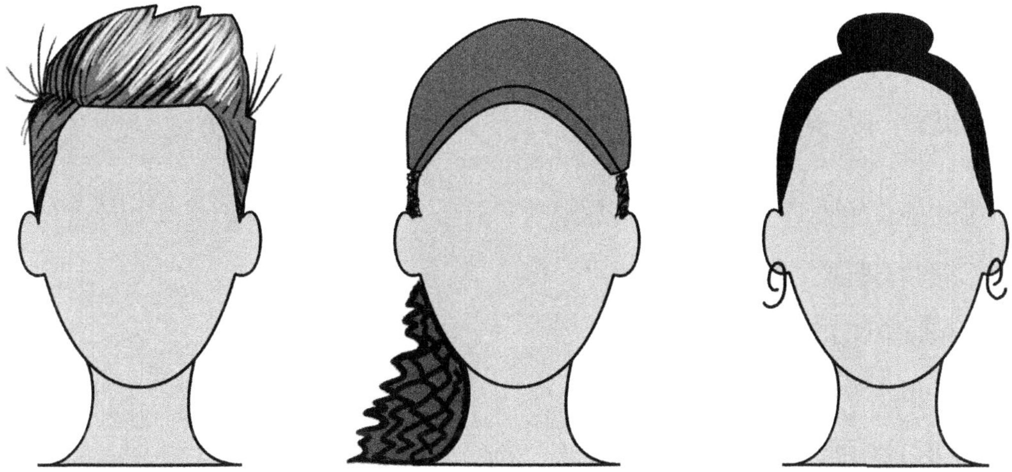

AUSTRALIA Women
*62 WT20I's (2009-18)*

WEST INDIES Women
*101 WT20I's (2014-24)*

SOUTH AFRICA Women
*127 WODI's (2007-22)*

# DIRECTION 86

Taking a letter from each segment of the circle in turn, can you spell out the name (8,8) of a West Indies women's cricketer (*45 WT20I's, 2011-16*). You need to find the starting points and identify the direction her first and last names are spelt.

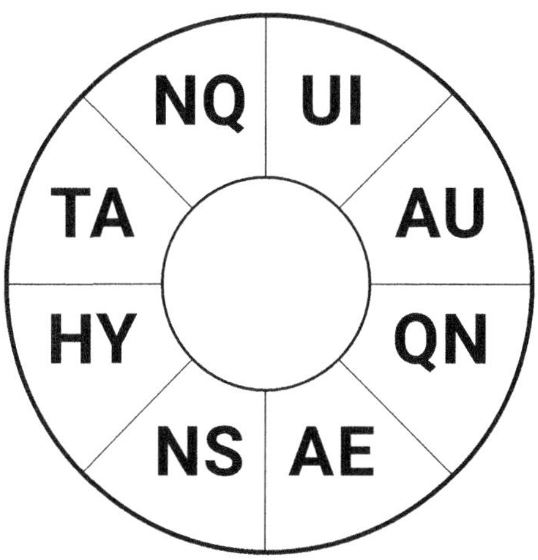


# VARIATION 87

Can you complete the grid so that every row and column contain each of the letters found in the surname of Mary-Anne **MUSONDA** (ZIM) (*58 WT20I's, 2019-24*)?

| | | | | | | |
|---|---|---|---|---|---|---|
| S | | | | | N | |
| | | D | | | | |
| | O | | | D | | M |
| U | | | | A | | |
| | | | N | | S | |
| | | | | O | | D |
| N | | | | | | O |

## MATCH UP 88

Can you transfer the following suffixes and nations to the list below to complete the names of five women's cricket teams and where they are based?

**THUNDER** ~~**GIANTS**~~ **ROYALS**

**DRAGONS** **MAGICIANS** **SCORCHERS**

*Australia* *West Indies* *England* *South Africa* ~~*India*~~ *New Zealand*

| | | |
|---|---|---|
| GUJARAT | **GIANTS** | *India* |
| CANTERBURY | ........................ | ........................ |
| BARBADOS | ........................ | ........................ |
| LANCASHIRE | ........................ | ........................ |
| NORTH WEST | ........................ | ........................ |
| PERTH | ........................ | ........................ |

## BUMP BALL 89

Can you identify the missing letters that complete the surnames of 6 Ireland women's cricketers?
Next, rearrange the missing letters to spell the surname of another Ireland women's cricketer (*6 WODI's, 2022-24*).

| | | | | | |
|---|---|---|---|---|---|
| ● | O | Y | L | A | N |
| O | L | E | A | ● | Y |
| M | ● | L | I | N | S |
| D | A | W | ● | O | N |
| C | O | ● | F | E | Y |
| L | I | T | T | L | ● |

## INSIDE OUT 90

Enter a word in the spaces of each row to spell a seven letter word. When complete the shaded squares will spell out the surname of a Brazil women's cricketer (*27 WT20I's, 2021-24*).

| | | | | | | |
|---|---|---|---|---|---|---|
| A | B | S | ▒ | | | D |
| E | M | | ▒ | | H | Y |
| F | | | ▒ | F | U | L |
| E | V | I | ▒ | | | T |
| I | N | | ▒ | | M | S |
| A | | | ▒ | I | V | E |
| I | L | | ▒ | | I | C |

# CRICTETRIS

Drop each of the shapes from the top of the grid to spell the surnames of ten England women's cricketers reading across. One of the shapes has been dropped to help you get started.

Note: The shapes should not be rotated or reflected and must be able to be dropped into the grid so that they come to rest on another shape or the grid bottom.

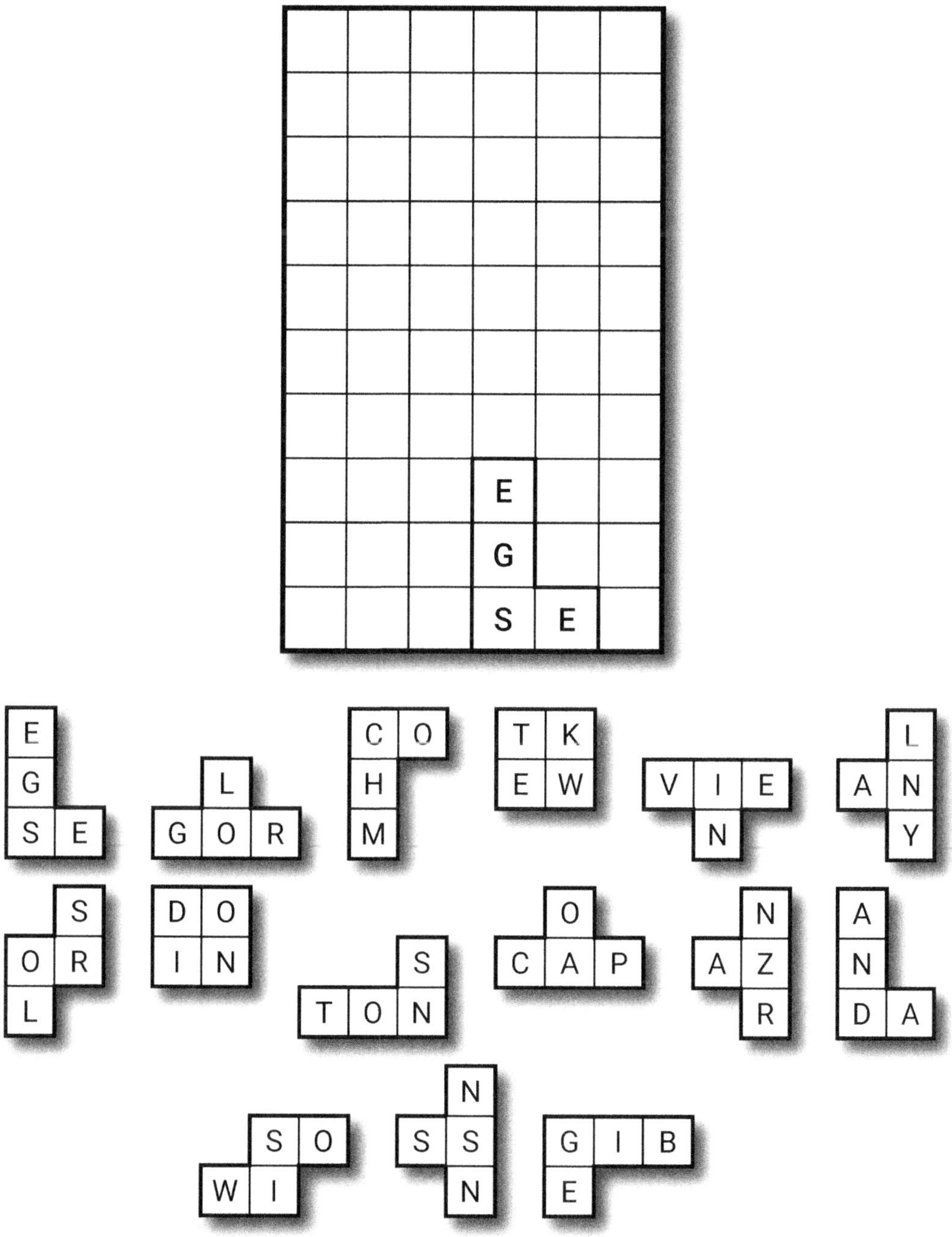

# WORDSEARCH



The surnames of the 20 cricketers who have scored the most runs for Netherlands Women in WT20I's are hidden in the Wordsearch below. Their names can be found horizontally (forwards and backwards), vertically (up or down) or diagonally. Can you find all 20 players?

| | | | | | | | | | | | | | | | |
|---|---|---|---|---|---|---|---|---|---|---|---|---|---|---|---|
| S | Q | A | R | I | N | D | S | I | L | A | K | V | Z | N | P |
| E | I | D | L | G | R | E | B | N | E | T | T | A | W | O | K |
| V | R | E | V | A | T | L | I | R | S | U | E | N | I | A | T |
| L | E | G | Z | P | N | J | W | O | L | A | K | O | L | U | R |
| T | E | R | W | H | M | S | P | Z | V | N | J | E | L | E | D |
| P | H | O | I | A | L | N | E | S | G | E | I | S | I | A | V |
| M | D | O | N | E | J | Y | A | R | D | B | R | E | N | E | S |
| S | N | T | M | I | R | L | T | E | J | L | M | D | G | L | O |
| V | A | I | R | S | O | P | E | G | I | G | R | A | I | E | T |
| E | L | K | J | M | O | L | K | E | N | B | O | E | R | J | D |
| R | G | Y | O | L | E | N | W | I | J | W | H | N | V | S | K |
| L | A | N | I | D | I | B | R | S | O | P | A | C | L | O | M |
| D | S | W | A | T | R | E | T | N | E | V | E | D | N | A | V |
| O | Z | V | R | L | V | I | F | A | K | L | W | C | O | Y | W |
| L | G | E | N | O | E | S | N | L | E | S | O | P | H | V | L |
| R | A | M | B | A | L | D | O | D | X | R | A | M | T | O | A |

Number of WT20I runs at 20 October 2024:

**DE GROOT** Carlijn (NED, *2008-11*) *66*
**DE LANGE** Caroline (NED, *2019-24*) *66*
**DE LEEDE** Babette (NED, *2018-24*) *927*
**KALIS** Sterre (NED, *2018-24*) *1,198*
**LANDHEER** Hannah (NED, *2019-24*) *51*
**LANSER** Esther (NED, *2010-11*) *104*
**LYNCH** Eva (NED, *2019-24*) *112*
**MOLKENBOER** Phebe (NED, *2023-24*) *168*
**NIJMAN** Marijn (NED, *2009-11*) *55*
**OVERDIJK** Frederique (NED, *2019-24*) *162*
**POST** Juliet (NED, *2018-22*) *101*
**RAMBALDO** Helmien (NED, *2008-11*) *154*
**RIJKE** Robine (NED, *2018-24*) *875*
**SALOMONS** Carolien (NED, *2008-11*) *59*
**SIEGERS** Heather (NED, *2018-24*) *794*
**THOMSON** Annemijn (NED, *2019-24*) *41*
**VAN DEVENTER** Denise (NED, *2008-19*) *307*
**VERINGMEIER** Miranda (NED, *2008-21*) *367*
**WATTENBERG** Violet (NED, *2008-11*) *146*
**ZWILLING** Iris (NED, *2019-24*) *622*

# SURNAMES



Each of the rows below contain the first names of 3 women's international cricketers who have the same surname. However, all the vowels have been removed. Can you identify the first names of each cricketer and shared surname? Enter the surname where shown to reveal the name of another cricketer (5,4) in the shaded boxes.

| | | | | | |
|---|---|---|---|---|---|
| CHuNTeLL | CAN | DeNiSe | AUS | KaTeY | NZ |
| DBB-NN | WI | GBY | IRE | M | NZ |
| CHRRY-NN | WI | KTHRN | SCO | LND | NZ |
| KY | ENG | KYLN | NAM | MDDY | NZ |
| LC | ARG | SRH | ENG | STFN | WI |
| JVR | PAK | RBY | BAN | YSMN | NAM |
| LC | WI | CL | AUS | BRYNY | ENG |
| MY | IRE | LS | MAL | JL | AUS |
| CHRRY-NN | WI | RNK | IND | RT | USA |

Name of cricketer: ........................................................................

## MISSING LETTERS 94

Working from letter to adjacent letter in any direction can you spell out the name of a Pakistan women's cricketer (*67 WODI's, 2017-24*)?
You need to find the starting point and identify the missing letters.

| | | |
|---|---|---|
| A | H | ? |
| S | N | A |
| U | N | S |
| ? | H | A |

## FIVE DOWN 95

Insert letters into the grid below to form five words reading across. When complete, the name of a South Africa women's cricketer (*23 WODI's, 1997-2002*) will be spelt out reading down the shaded squares.

| | | | | |
|---|---|---|---|---|
| S | | I | | L |
| C | | D | | R |
| T | | A | | N |
| F | | O | | T |
| S | | E | | E |

## END TO END RUN 96

Can you get from wicket **A** to wicket **B** without travelling through any of the **X** squares – then make your way back to **A** by avoiding the **O** squares?

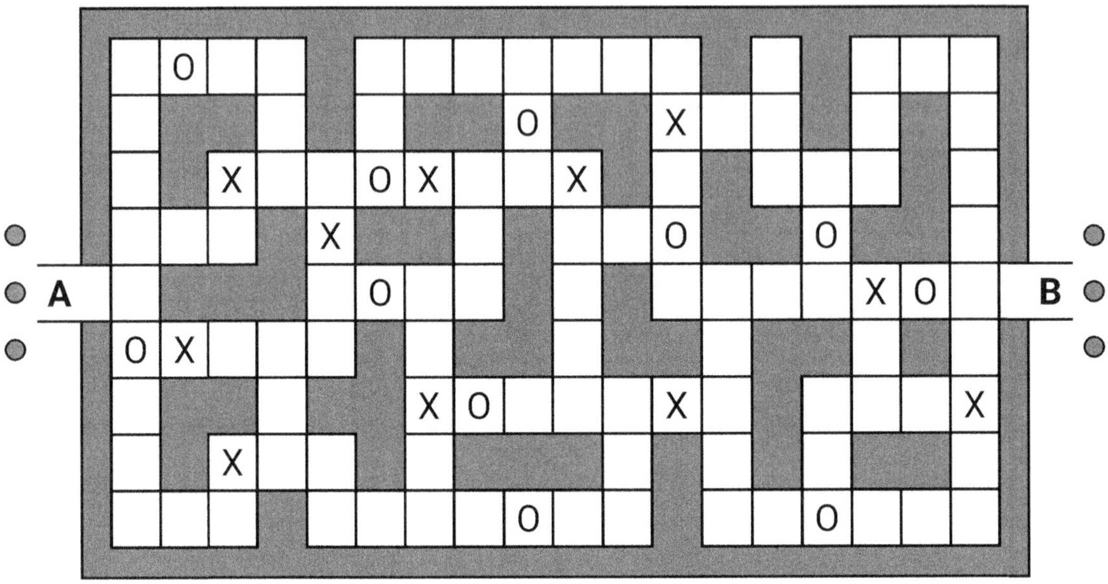

## DO YOU KNOW? 97

The inaugural Women's Cricket World Cup in 1973 was contested by seven teams, including four of the teams listed below.
Can you name the team that was not a participant?

A. Bahamas
B. International XI
C. Jamaica
D. Trinidad and Tobago
E. Young England

## CONNECTION? 98

The women's international cricketers listed below have something unusual in common. Can you spot what it is?

Erica RENDLER (USA)
Rachel OVERMAN (IOM)
Samantha LOBATTO (IND)
Krima KAPADIA (CAN)
Bernadine BEZUIDENHOUT (NZ)

## CONUNDRUM 99

Can you unscramble the anagram to reveal the name of an England women's cricketer?

**A SILK CONTAINER** (ENG) (*58 WODI's, 2001-10*)

# LOGIC PUZZLE



England Women are playing a fantasy WODI match against West Indies Women. From the information below can you work out how each of England's top and middle order batters lost their wicket, off whose bowling and how many runs they scored?

**Clues:**

1. Alice Capsey scored 47, thus scoring more runs than Heather Knight, who lost her wicket off the bowling of Shamilia Connell.
2. One of the England openers lost their wicket to Karishma Ramharack after making 61 runs. Nat Sciver-Brunt, who was out lbw, scored more than 3 runs.
3. The England batter who lost her wicket to Zaida James scored fewer runs than her team-mate caught at long-off. The batter who made a century was stumped, but scored more runs than Tammy Beaumont.
4. Hayley Matthews clean bowled one of the England batters with a brilliant yorker.

| | Bowled | Caught | Caught & bowled | LBW | Stumped | Connell | Fletcher | James | Matthews | Ramharack | 3 | 29 | 47 | 61 | 102 |
|---|---|---|---|---|---|---|---|---|---|---|---|---|---|---|---|
| Tammy Beaumont | | | | | | | | | | | | | | | |
| Maia Bouchier | | | | | | | | | | | | | | | |
| Alice Capsey | | | | | | | | | | | | | | | |
| Heather Knight | | | | | | | | | | | | | | | |
| Nat Sciver-Brunt | | | | | | | | | | | | | | | |
| 3 | | | | | | | | | | | | | | | |
| 29 | | | | | | | | | | | | | | | |
| 47 | | | | | | | | | | | | | | | |
| 61 | | | | | | | | | | | | | | | |
| 102 | | | | | | | | | | | | | | | |
| Shamilia Connell | | | | | | | | | | | | | | | |
| Afy Fletcher | | | | | | | | | | | | | | | |
| Zaida James | | | | | | | | | | | | | | | |
| Hayley Matthews | | | | | | | | | | | | | | | |
| Karishma Ramharack | | | | | | | | | | | | | | | |

Tip: Use the grid to record all the positive or negative facts obtained from the clues. By placing a tick or cross in the relevant squares of the grid, and cross-referencing the clues, you will be able to work out all the correct facts.

| BATTER | HOW OUT | BOWLER | RUNS SCORED |
|---|---|---|---|
| | | | |
| | | | |
| | | | |
| | | | |
| | | | |

# WAGON WHEEL **101**

How many words of four or more letters can you make from the letters on the wheel. Each word must include the central letter and other letters may only be used once. Plurals, foreign words and proper nouns are not eligible. See if you can find the nine letter word that is a fundamental part of playing cricket, whether as a beginner or an experienced player.

Target: 12 words = GOOD, 24 words = EXCELLENT, 36 words = OUTSTANDING

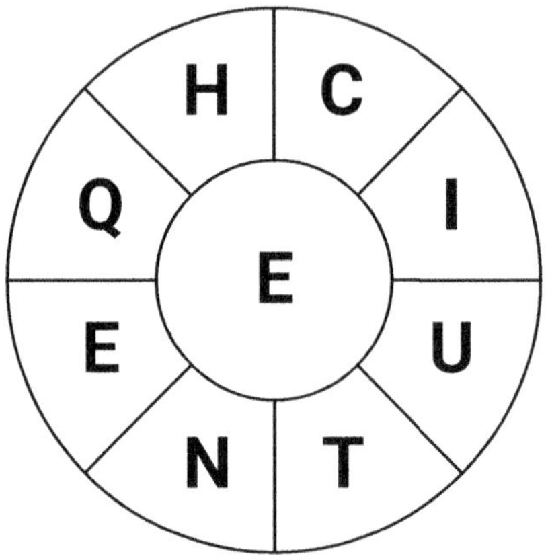


# CRYPTOGRAM **102**

An amusing quote by a former women's international cricketer (*30 WODI's, 2014-17*) has been encrypted by replacing each letter of the alphabet with another. The cricketer was talking about her new-born son who has dual nationality. We've started to decipher the quote but can you finish it off and also reveal who said it?

| Z | W | | L | C | ' | A | | H | T | T | F | | X | P | | A | Y | T | E | P | , | | L | T | Y | C | - | |
|---|---|---|---|---|---|---|---|---|---|---|---|---|---|---|---|---|---|---|---|---|---|---|---|---|---|---|---|---|
| | | | | | ' | | | | | | | | | | | | | | R | | , | | | | | | - | |

| W | D | S | S | J | | L | C | | Y | S | X | J | A | | W | T | E | | X | D | A | P | E | X | S | Z | X | . |
|---|---|---|---|---|---|---|---|---|---|---|---|---|---|---|---|---|---|---|---|---|---|---|---|---|---|---|---|---|
| | | | | Y | | | | | | | | Y | | | | | R | | | | | | R | | | | | . |

| Z | W | | L | C | ' | A | | O | T | P | , | | L | C | | M | X | O | | Y | S | X | J | | W | T | E | |
|---|---|---|---|---|---|---|---|---|---|---|---|---|---|---|---|---|---|---|---|---|---|---|---|---|---|---|---|---|
| | | | | | ' | | | | | | , | | | | | | | | | | | | Y | | | | R | |

| C | O | H | S | X | O | F | . |
|---|---|---|---|---|---|---|---|
| | | | | | | | . |

| B | E | Z | A | P | C | O | | K | C | X | V | A |
|---|---|---|---|---|---|---|---|---|---|---|---|---|
| | R | | | | | | | | | | | |

## MIXED UP PAIRS

**103**

Can you rearrange the pairs of letters to spell the name of a UAE women's cricketer *(88 WT20I's, 2018-24)*?

| GE | SH | GO | DA | VI | AE | KA |
|---|---|---|---|---|---|---|

## CRICKET (DING)BATS

**104**

Can you identify the cricket-related terms suggested by the images below?

| *Omit* | *Add* |
|---|---|
| WRAP UP | DISCONTINUE |
| FINISH | CLIMAX |
| CONCLUDE | WIND-UP |
| OVER | FINALE |

1. ..................................................

2. ..................................................

## TAILENDERS

**105**

The name of a Pakistan women's cricketer (*24 WODI's, 1997-2004*) can be inserted in the bottom row of the grid below to complete nine 3-letter words reading downwards. Can you identify them?

| B | S | L | S | T | J | E | O | P |
|---|---|---|---|---|---|---|---|---|
| U | P | I | K | E | O | M | A | I |
| | | | | | | | | |

# PITCH IT UP 106

Enter the letters into their correct boxes in the vertical columns above to reveal the name of a women's international cricketer, their national team and four domestic teams they have played for around the cricket world.

| | | | | | | ■ | | | | | | | ■ | ■ | ■ | ■ |
|---|---|---|---|---|---|---|---|---|---|---|---|---|---|---|---|---|
| | | | ■ | | | | | | | | ■ | ■ | ■ | ■ | ■ | ■ |
| | | | | | | | ■ | | | | | | | | | S |
| | | | | | ■ | | | | | | | | ■ | ■ | ■ | ■ |
| | | | | | | ■ | | | | | | | | | | S |
| | | | | | | | | ■ | ■ | ■ | ■ | ■ | ■ | ■ | ■ | ■ |
| H | O | C | M | R | E | R | L | C | I | D | S | R | A | C | E | ~~S~~ |
| T | E | B | H | A | N | A | P | A | R | E | T | T | I | N | T | ~~S~~ |
| R | A | W | A | Z | T | I | A | U | K | E | I | S | | | | |
| T | E | S | N | T | A | L | O | D | I | R | T | C | | | | |
| N | R | E | T | E | L | | H | R | N | S | | | | | | |
| C | A | N | | R | | | | | | | | | | | | |

# MISSING LETTERS 107

Working from letter to adjacent letter in any direction can you spell out the name of an India women's cricketer (*53 WT20I's, 2018-22*)?
You need to find the starting point and identify the missing letters.

| ? | A | ? |
|---|---|---|
| N | A | T |
| I | A | H |
| ? | A | ? |

# RECORD HOLDER 108

Amelia Kerr (NZ) (*75 WODI's, 2016-24*) holds the record for the highest individual score in a Women's ODI match.

Amelia set the record on 13 June 2018 playing for New Zealand Women against Ireland Women at the YMCA Cricket Club, Dublin. How many runs did Amelia score?

A. 175 not out
B. 184 not out
C. 232 not out
D. 263 not out

# CRICKET CODEWORD

**109**

Each number in the grid represents a different letter of the alphabet. Can you complete the grid correctly and identify the reference to women's international cricket in the shaded squares?

| | | | | | | | | | | | | |
|---|---|---|---|---|---|---|---|---|---|---|---|---|
| 10 | 24 | 19 | 11 | 1 | 23 | | 22 | 16 | 26 | 17 | 18 | 9 |
| 8 | | 8 | | 11 | | 15 | | 25 | | 18 | | 16 |
| 22 | 10 | 14 | 8 | 11 | 19 | 8 | | 4 | 19 | 8 | 1 | 23 |
| 26 | | 8 | | 18 | | 3 | | 10 | | 26 | | 2 |
| 19 | 10 | 9 | 12 | | 4 | 21 | 16 | 14 | 22 | 11 | 18 | 15 |
| 11 | | | | 15 | | 2 | | 10 | | 22 | | |
| 7 | 8 | 4 | 6 | 16 | 9 | | 10 | 2 | 11 | 1 | 8 | 4 |
| | | 21 | | 10 | | 2 | | 16 | | | | 10 |
| 5 | 17 | 16 | 15 | 2 | 8 | 11 | 18 | | 13 | 11 | 23 | 15 |
| 17 | | 10 | | 23 | | 25 | | 20 | | 17 | | 4 |
| 10 | 24 | 24 | 19 | 16 | | 8 | 18 | 16 | 22 | 2 | 8 | 10 |
| 4 | | 16 | | 19 | | 4 | | 15 | | 9 | | 9 |
| 6 | 10 | 22 | 10 | 2 | 16 | | 15 | 2 | 22 | 11 | 6 | 16 |

A B C D E F G H I J K L M N O P Q R S T U V W X Y Z

| 1 | 2 | 3 | 4 | 5 | 6 | 7 | 8 | 9 | 10 | 11 | 12 | 13 |
|---|---|---|---|---|---|---|---|---|---|---|---|---|
| M | | | | | K | | | | | | | |
| 14 | 15 | 16 | 17 | 18 | 19 | 20 | 21 | 22 | 23 | 24 | 25 | 26 |
| | | | | | | | | | | | | |

# MIXED UP THREE'S

**110**

Can you rearrange the groups of letters to spell the name of an international women's cricketer *(6 WODI's, 2018-23)*?

| CHA | DSO | ALI | RDS | AVI | CED | NRI |
|---|---|---|---|---|---|---|

# WORDSEARCH



The one-word names or suffixes of 20 women's cricket teams from around the world have been hidden in the Wordsearch below. The names can be found written horizontally (forwards and backwards), vertically (up or down) or diagonally. How many can you find?

| | | | | | | | | | | | | | | | |
|---|---|---|---|---|---|---|---|---|---|---|---|---|---|---|---|
| T | S | F | O | A | U | S | V | P | S | R | E | X | I | S | L |
| E | Y | I | V | H | T | I | B | D | O | W | L | O | R | H | M |
| O | C | R | Y | E | D | G | L | Y | T | A | E | K | S | U | T |
| D | I | A | K | A | S | T | A | R | S | R | O | R | N | C | H |
| E | Y | C | P | T | N | L | S | O | L | R | E | U | A | S | O |
| I | O | D | A | I | S | K | N | D | I | G | S | P | T | E | D |
| R | S | R | S | E | T | I | M | A | N | Y | D | R | I | S | I |
| S | E | A | N | I | H | A | B | E | Q | A | I | M | T | O | A |
| Y | N | G | B | R | S | N | L | T | P | B | T | O | K | D | M |
| J | A | O | S | L | W | L | A | S | H | U | R | Z | R | A | O |
| E | C | N | O | R | A | E | O | H | P | M | O | A | U | F | N |
| T | I | S | G | H | N | Z | L | S | R | E | P | I | V | C | D |
| B | R | A | C | E | P | B | E | I | U | S | D | O | G | E | S |
| E | R | N | I | B | C | Y | V | H | O | W | K | I | T | A | R |
| D | U | Y | M | O | U | N | T | A | I | N | E | E | R | S | M |
| L | H | D | R | S | I | X | O | R | O | C | S | C | U | K | E |

1. ..............................
2. ..............................
3. ..............................
4. ..............................
5. ..............................
6. ..............................
7. ..............................
8. ..............................
9. ..............................
10. ..............................
11. ..............................
12. ..............................
13. ..............................
14. ..............................
15. ..............................
16. ..............................
17. ..............................
18. ..............................
19. ..............................
20. ..............................

## CRICKET CIRCLES 112

Replace the question marks with letters so that the letters in each circle can be arranged to spell the surnames of three women's cricketers who all play for the same national team. Can you name the cricketers and the team?

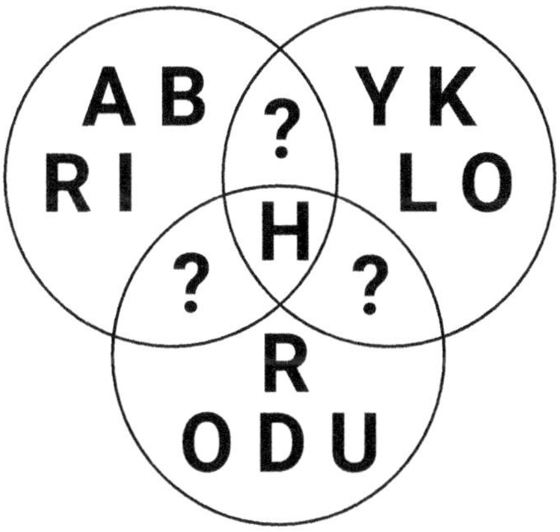


## MIDDLE ORDER 113

Arrange the letters found in **PUNAM RAUT** (IND) (*73 WODI's, 2009-21*) in the grid below to form six five-letter words reading across and down.

**P U N A M R A U T**

| | | | | |
|---|---|---|---|---|
| | T | H | S | |
| E | | | | T |
| P | | | | S |
| S | | | | D |
| | H | N | K | |

## PARTNERSHIP 114

For each of the word pairs listed, identify the 5-letter word (and surname of a women's international cricketer) that can be placed after the first word and before the second word to make two new words or phrases. Enter your answers in the grid and rearrange the shaded letters to reveal the name of an ICC Associate member.

| | | | | | | | | |
|---|---|---|---|---|---|---|---|---|
| VILLAGE .................. CARD | | | | (shaded) | | NZ (*2012-24*) |
| LAUGHING ............. PROOF | | | (shaded) | | | ENG (*1992-96*) |
| EGG ............................ LIE | | (shaded) | | | | SCO (*2001-03*) |
| AIR ......................... AWAY | | | (shaded) | | | HK (*2021-24*) |
| RAZOR ................ TONGUE | (shaded) | | | | | IRE (*1997-2000*) |
| BRAIN ...................... PLAY | | (shaded) | | | | WI (*1993-2005*) |
| CUT ......................... FUSE | | | | | (shaded) | NAM (*2019*) |

**Name of ICC member:** ..........................................................

## CROSSWORD 4s

**115**

Can you complete the puzzle by correctly placing the four-letter cricket-related words into the crossword?

TEST CALL RAIN STOP TEAM EDGE LOST FLAT SPIN TIME
KEEP RUNS TIES MISS BOWL TRAP CORK OPEN LEAP BATS

---

## BOX CLEVER

**116**

Can you shade-in some of the boxes in the grid below to reveal something connected with Anya Shrubsole (ENG) (*86 WODI's, 2008-22*)? First, shade-in all the boxes containing the letter **A**. Then, shade-in all the boxes that contain one other letter found in **ANYA SHRUBSOLE**'s name to spell out the connection in the grid.

Tip: Use a pencil to fully shade-in the relevant boxes.

| H | N | U | B | E |  | A | O | H | N | Y | L | S | E | B | R |
|---|---|---|---|---|---|---|---|---|---|---|---|---|---|---|---|
| E | L | H | R | N | O | N | A | Y | S | U | R | B |  | O | L |
| S | A | Y |  | B | A | O |  | R | H | L | N | E | A | U | Y |
| Y |  | O | A | L | R | S | N | U | O |  | A | H | O |  | B |
| R | O | E |  | Y | N | U | H | L | A | B |  | U | A | Y | S |
| B | H | S | U | R | S | E | Y | B |  | A | O | R | L | N | E |

## CRIDOKU 117

Fill in the squares of the grid so that each row, each column and each smaller 3x3 block contains all the letters which spell **SHARYN BOW** (AUS) (*11 WODI's, 1993-94*) only once.

| | | | | | | | | |
|---|---|---|---|---|---|---|---|---|
| | H | | | | | B | | |
| | | Y | B | | H | | | W |
| B | | | | | A | | R | |
| | S | H | N | | O | | Y | |
| | | | | A | | | | |
| | N | | H | | S | O | B | |
| | Y | | R | | | | | O |
| O | | | W | | B | H | | |
| | | N | | | | | S | |

## SIX DOWN 118

Insert letters into the grid below to form six words reading across. When complete, the name of a Pakistan women's cricketer (*30 WT20I's 2020-23*) will be spelt out reading down the shaded squares.

| | | | | |
|---|---|---|---|---|
| F | | I | | T |
| B | | L | | W |
| V | | R | | E |
| A | | K | | D |
| S | | E | | P |
| M | | G | | A |

## ROTATION 119

Find the starting point and fill in the blanks to reveal the name (6,10) of an Ireland women's cricketer (*75 WT20I's, 2008-24*). Only alternate letters are shown.

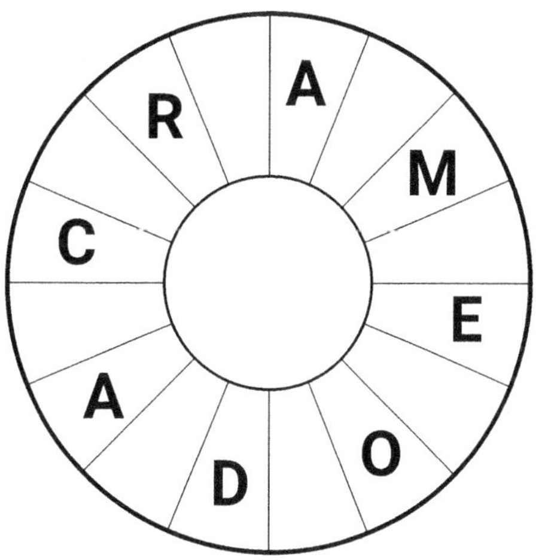

## FOURS 120

Can you identify the West Indies women's cricketer (*12 WODI's, 2008-10*) whose surname can be placed before PRINT, WONDER, HOURS and TALK to make two new words or phrases?

**PRINT**
**WONDER**
**HOURS**
**TALK**

## HIT FOR SIX 121

Complete the grid so that every row and column, and every outlined area, contains each of the letters found in the surname of Rachael **HAYNES** (AUS) (*77 WODI's, 2009-22*).

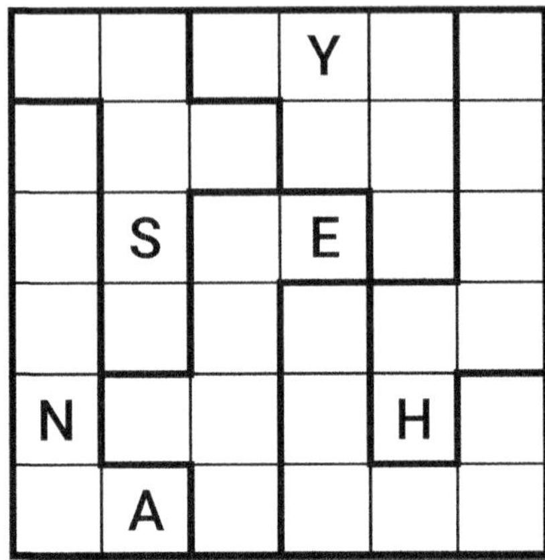


## TWINS 122

The names of five pairs of twins who have played women's international cricket are mixed up in the box below along with their national teams. Can you match up the names and teams as appropriate?

KATE West Indies **Signal**
**Ireland** Kyshona *JOYCE*
JANE BLACKWELL Liz
Rose ***Isobel*** ENGLAND
**NEW ZEALAND** Kycia
**Alex** Jill **KNIGHT**
Powell **AUSTRALIA** *Cecilia*

1. .................... .................... .................................... ....................................
2. .................... .................... .................................... ....................................
3. .................... .................... .................................... ....................................
4. .................... .................... .................................... ....................................
5. .................... .................... .................................... ....................................

# FOLLOW ON



Every answer to each clue (except the first) starts with the last letter of the preceding answer, and when entered into the grid follows a spiral path reading anti-clockwise to the centre. When complete, the shaded diagonal squares will spell out the name of a women's international cricketer and a domestic team they have played for.

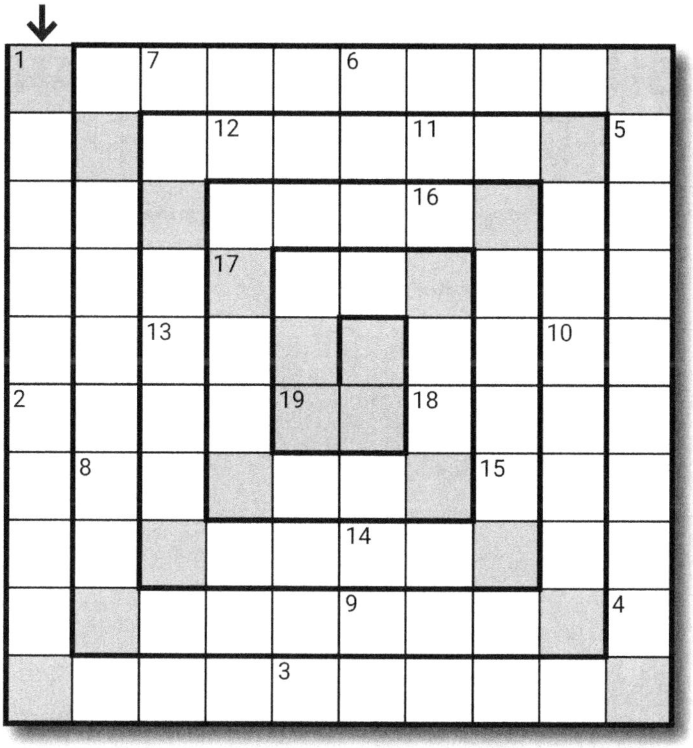

1. A small, portable computer that can be easily carried (6)
2. Of supreme importance (9)
3. Hitched a lift in a passing vehicle; well-worn pages in a book (7)
4. Dead, flaky skin on the scalp and in hair (8)
5. Get to the bottom of; understand (6)
6. A list of food and drinks in a cafe or restaurant (4)
7. The whole of space including stars, planets, galaxies, etc (8)
8. Hires someone for work in exchange for payment (7)
9. A person's assistant or close associate, considered as a subordinate (8)
10. A chess piece (6)
11. Journey or excursion, especially one for pleasure (4)
12. Dish of Italian origin, consisting of a flat baked bread with toppings (5)
13. Extreme pain, suffering or distress (7)
14. The handle of a sword or dagger (4)
15. A natural ability or aptitude in a particular field (6)
16. Double in degree or quantity (5)
17. Investigates, looks at closely (8)
18. Utensil with broad, flat blade for various purposes (7)
19. The whole of; everyone (3)

# PAIR UP 124

The 4-letter surnames of seven Pakistan women's cricketers are jumbled up in the grid below. Can you match the pair of letters and work out which pair is not used?

| IN | RA | AN | QI | NA |
|---|---|---|---|---|
| SH | AM | RI | BA | AH |
| AZ | IG | SA | KH | UF |

# CRICKET (DING)BATS 125

Can you identify the cricket-related terms suggested by the images below?

**→ CALM ←**
**DISCIPLINE**
**PEACE**
**COMMAND**

1. ..............................................

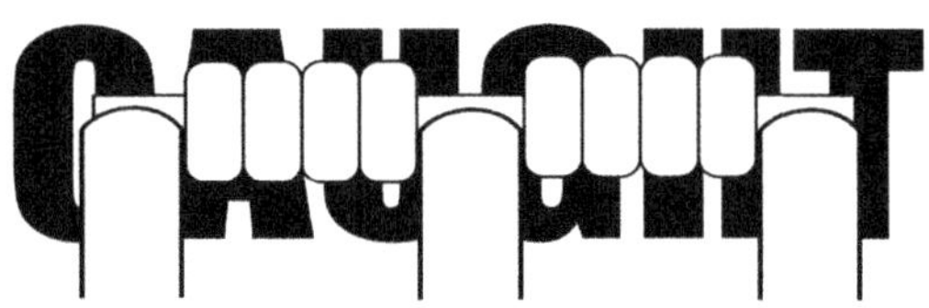


2. ..............................................

# CONUNDRUM 126

Can you unscramble the anagram to reveal the name of an Australia women's cricketer?

**A BRIDE CROWN** (AUS) (*34 WT20I's, 2021-24*)

# CRICKET CROSSWORD

## ACROSS

1. Cricket team based in Bulawayo, Zimbabwe, captained by Nomvelo Sibanda (7)
4. Ayabonga .........., South Africa medium-pace bowler (*103 WODI's, 2012-24*) (5)
6. Melbourne .........., WBBL cricket team captained by Annabel Sutherland (5)
8. The average total scored per over (3-4)
10. .......... Raack, Ireland all-rounder born in Australia (*22 WT20I's, 2018-22*) (7)
11. .......... Guha, England bowler, now TV & radio broadcaster (*83 WODI's, 2001-11*) (3)
14. An official who enforces the rules and adjudicates play (6)
16. The Hallyburton Johnstone .........., women's one-day cricket competition in New Zealand (6)
18. Emma .........., Perth Scorchers and Hong Kong medium-pace bowler (*29 WT20I's, 2019-24*) (3)
19. .......... Province, women's cricket team based in Cape Town, South Africa (7)
23. The legal method of bowling in cricket (7)
24. see 20 down (5)
25. Bowling style employed by pace bowlers to create movement on the ball (5)
26. Used in cricket format at 1 down (3,4)

## DOWN

1. .......... match, longest form of international cricket (4)
2. During play, a cricket ball can be replaced if it loses this quality (5)
3. .......... Mandhana, RCB and India top-order batter (*145 WT20I's, 2013-24*) (6)
4. Alana .........., Perth Scorchers and Australia leg-spin bowler (*29 WODI's, 2022-24*) (4)
5. And 22 Down: Sports stadium and cricket venue in the state of South Australia (8)
7. .......... Kalis, Netherlands top-order batter (*38 WT20I's, 2018-24*) (6)
9. .......... Tector, Ireland all-rounder and medium-pace bowler (*5 WODI's, 2024*) (5)
12. A bowling delivery that reaches the batter without bouncing (4,4)
13. Trisha .........., South Africa wicket-keeper, holds record for highest number of WODI dismissals (*134 WODI's, 2007-22*) (6)
15. Award presented to winners of cricket tournament or Player of the Match (5)
17. Similar to 12 down - but a delivery which reaches the batter above waist height (6)
20. and 24 across: India left-arm spinner (*81 WT20I's, 2018-24*) (5)
21. Diana .........., Pakistan medium-pace bowler (*57 WODI's, 2015-24*) (4)
22. See 5 down (4)

## MIDDLE ORDER 128

Arrange the letters found in **ELENA TICE** (IRE) (*25 WT20I's, 2011-15*) in the grid below to form six five-letter words reading across and down.

ELENA TICE

|   | R | K | M |   |
|---|---|---|---|---|
| G |   |   |   | S |
| S |   |   |   | E |
| D |   |   |   | D |
|   | C | K | R |   |

## MID-OFF 129

Can you identify the West Indies women's cricketer (*70 WODI's, 2008-17*) whose surname fits in the sequence of words below?

**ALE**
**LEAD**
**?????**
**PLAYED**
**ENDPLAY**

## ODD ONE OUT 130

Can you identify which one of the following facts is NOT true about India women's cricketer Smriti Mandhana?

**SMRITI MANDHANA**
**INDIA WOMEN**
*145 WT20I's: 3,568 runs*

A. Smriti started playing cricket at the age of two. When she was just 9 years old, she was picked in Maharashtra state's U15 team and at 11 years old, picked in the U19 team.

B. Smriti made her international debut on 5 April 2013 at the age of 16 years and 266 days. In only her second international appearance, she scored a century - becoming the youngest-ever WODI centurion.

C. She is the first-ever cricketer to score 10 consecutive 50+ scores in ODI's while on the chasing team.

D. She has been the recipient of numerous ICC awards, including the Rachael Heyhoe-Flint Award in both 2018 and 2021 for being best female cricketer.

## STAIRCASE 131

Arrange the surnames of the seven New Zealand women's cricketers listed below so that when placed in the horizontal rows of the grid, the letters of the diagonal 'staircase' spell out an eighth cricketer (NZ, *73 WODI's, 2012-20*).

BROWNE HOCKLEY GREEN PULFORD LEWIS SCRIPPS BEVEGE

---

## CRICKET GROUNDS 132

Can you match the following cricket grounds to the correct location? All the grounds have played host to numerous women's international cricket matches.

| | |
|---|---|
| EDEN GARDENS | *Wellington, New Zealand* |
| BUFFALO PARK | *Lahore, Pakistan* |
| ALLAN BORDER FIELD | *East London, South Africa* |
| NEW ROAD | *Dubai, United Arab Emirates* |
| GADDAFI STADIUM | *Kolkata, India* |
| CASTLE AVENUE | *Colombo, Sri Lanka* |
| BASIN RESERVE | *Bridgetown, Barbados* |
| ICC ACADEMY | *Worcester, England* |
| SINHALESE SPORTS CLUB | *Brisbane, Australia* |
| KENSINGTON OVAL | *Dublin, Ireland* |

# WORDSEARCH



The surnames of the 20 wicket-keepers who have taken the most career dismissals in WODI's have been hidden in the Wordsearch below. Their names can be found horizontally (forwards and backwards), vertically (up or down) or diagonally. Can you find all 20 players?

| | | | | | | | | | | | | | | | |
|---|---|---|---|---|---|---|---|---|---|---|---|---|---|---|---|
| A | X | S | M | I | J | E | F | I | R | P | N | R | N | A | M |
| W | G | T | A | O | R | O | L | L | S | F | O | I | M | S | Q |
| J | A | U | N | H | W | T | N | A | I | L | V | W | A | P | C |
| C | H | E | T | A | M | R | J | E | Y | M | E | S | R | J | N |
| P | S | B | L | D | Z | A | W | A | N | A | R | D | I | S | A |
| R | A | D | A | G | U | M | T | J | I | D | N | A | E | H | R |
| I | S | M | I | T | P | A | U | S | T | O | E | M | L | V | O |
| E | G | A | L | J | O | N | R | I | R | J | S | C | L | E | B |
| S | J | M | F | D | A | O | M | D | A | E | K | A | I | N | A |
| T | W | R | T | I | L | D | L | I | M | S | H | Z | U | R | T |
| H | A | E | K | S | E | A | K | F | R | E | D | N | G | V | P |
| M | L | V | H | J | W | R | O | L | A | J | H | L | A | H | S |
| O | A | B | A | T | O | A | C | H | E | T | T | Y | E | M | O |
| K | T | Y | S | I | T | M | I | B | P | R | I | A | J | I | N |
| J | A | I | N | R | W | A | L | S | E | U | L | M | S | Y | F |
| T | M | S | F | P | N | S | M | V | I | Y | O | T | A | B | I |

Number of wicket-keeper dismissals in WODI's at 20 October 2024:

**AGUILLEIRA** Merissa (WI, *2008-18*) *102*
**BATOOL FATIMA** (PAK, *2001-14*) *97*
**CHETTY** Trisha (SA, *2007-22*) *182*
**FIELDS** Jodie (AUS, *2006-13*) *74*
**HEALY** Alyssa (AUS, *2010-24*) *107*
**JAIN** Anju (IND, *1993-2005*) *81*
**JAIN** Karuna (IND, *2004-14*) *58*
**JONES** Amy (ENG, *2013-24*) *85*
**MANODARA** Dilani (SL, *2006-19*) *61*
**MARTIN** Katey (NZ, *2003-22*) *75*
**MATTHEWS** Christina (AUS, *1984-95*) *49*
**NAIK** Sulakshana (IND, *2002-13*) *60*
**PRICE** Julia (AUS, *1996-2005*) *99*
**PRIEST** Rachel (NZ, *2007-20*) *93*
**ROLLS** Rebecca (NZ, *1997-2007*) *133*
**SIDRA NAWAZ** (PAK, *2014-23*) *60*
**SMIT** Jane (ENG, *1993-2007*) *114*
**TAYLOR** Sarah (ENG, *2006-19*) *136*
**VERMA** Sushma (IND, *2014-21*) *49*
**WALDRON** Mary (IRE, *2010-23*) *49*

# SIXERS 134

The arrows in this grid indicate that the number on the next ball is lower. Can you complete the grid so that all rows and columns contain the numbers 1 to 6?

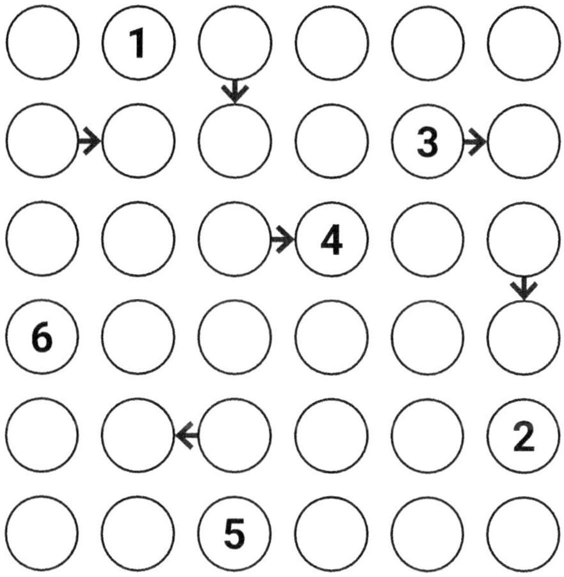


# INSIDE OUT 135

Enter a word in the spaces of each row to spell a seven letter word. When complete the shaded squares will spell out the surname of a Vanuatu women's cricketer (*34 WT20I's, 2019-24*).

| | | | | | | |
|---|---|---|---|---|---|---|
| C | L | I | | | | E |
| V | A | | | | C | Y |
| U | | | | D | E | D |
| M | E | S | | | | E |
| O | C | | | | O | N |
| T | | | | E | T | S |
| R | O | | | | T | E |

# DIRECTION 136

Taking a letter from each segment of the circle in turn, can you spell out the name of an Australia women's cricketer (*75 WT20I's, 2008-24*). They are the only-ever player to keep wicket, open the batting and captain in a Women's Test match.

You need to find the starting points and identify the direction the cricketer's first and last names are spelt.

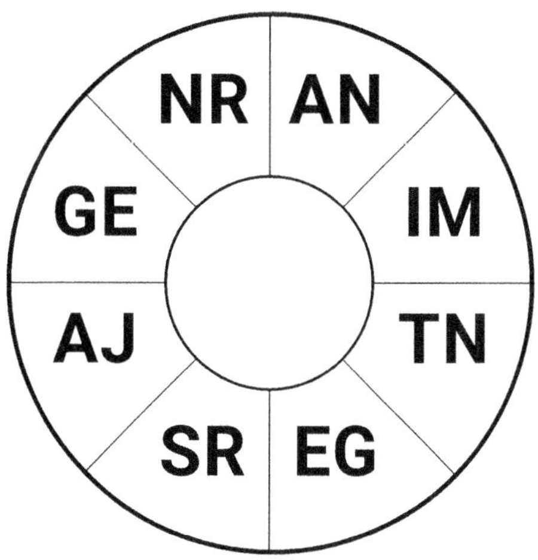

## VARIATION 137

Can you complete the grid so that every row and column contain each of the letters found in the surname of Sophia **DUNKLEY** (ENG) (*58 WT20I's, 2018-24*)?

| | | | | | | |
|---|---|---|---|---|---|---|
| | Y | | L | | | E |
| | | N | | | | |
| | | K | Y | | | |
| N | | | | U | K | |
| U | | | | | N | |
| | | | E | | | Y |
| | | | | | D | |

## BUMP BALL 138

Can you identify the missing letters that complete the surnames of 5 India women's cricketers?
Next, rearrange the missing letters to spell the surname of another India women's cricketer (*63 WODI's, 2011-22*).

| | | | | |
|---|---|---|---|---|
| A | | U | J | A |
| | A | D | H | U |
| P | U | N | | A |
| D | H | R | U | |
| P | A | | I | L |

## NAME BOGGLER 139

The surnames (or last names) of 11 cricketers who were squad members of the teams that played in the 2024 ICC Women's T20 World Cup are hidden in the grid below. How many surnames can you find?
Each name can only be spelt by moving from letter to adjacent letter, including diagonally. No individual letter can be used more than once in each name. Players sharing the same name only count as one.

Target:
4 cricketers = GOOD, 7 cricketers = EXCELLENT, 10 cricketers = OUTSTANDING

| | | | |
|---|---|---|---|
| Y | B | U | M |
| E | R | A | K |
| H | N | I | L |
| D | G | T | S |

# SUPER CRICTETRIS



Drop each of the shapes from the top of the grid to spell the surnames of ten women's international cricketers reading across. One of the shapes has been dropped to help you get started.
Note: The shapes should not be rotated or reflected and must be able to be dropped into the grid so that they come to rest on another shape or grid bottom.

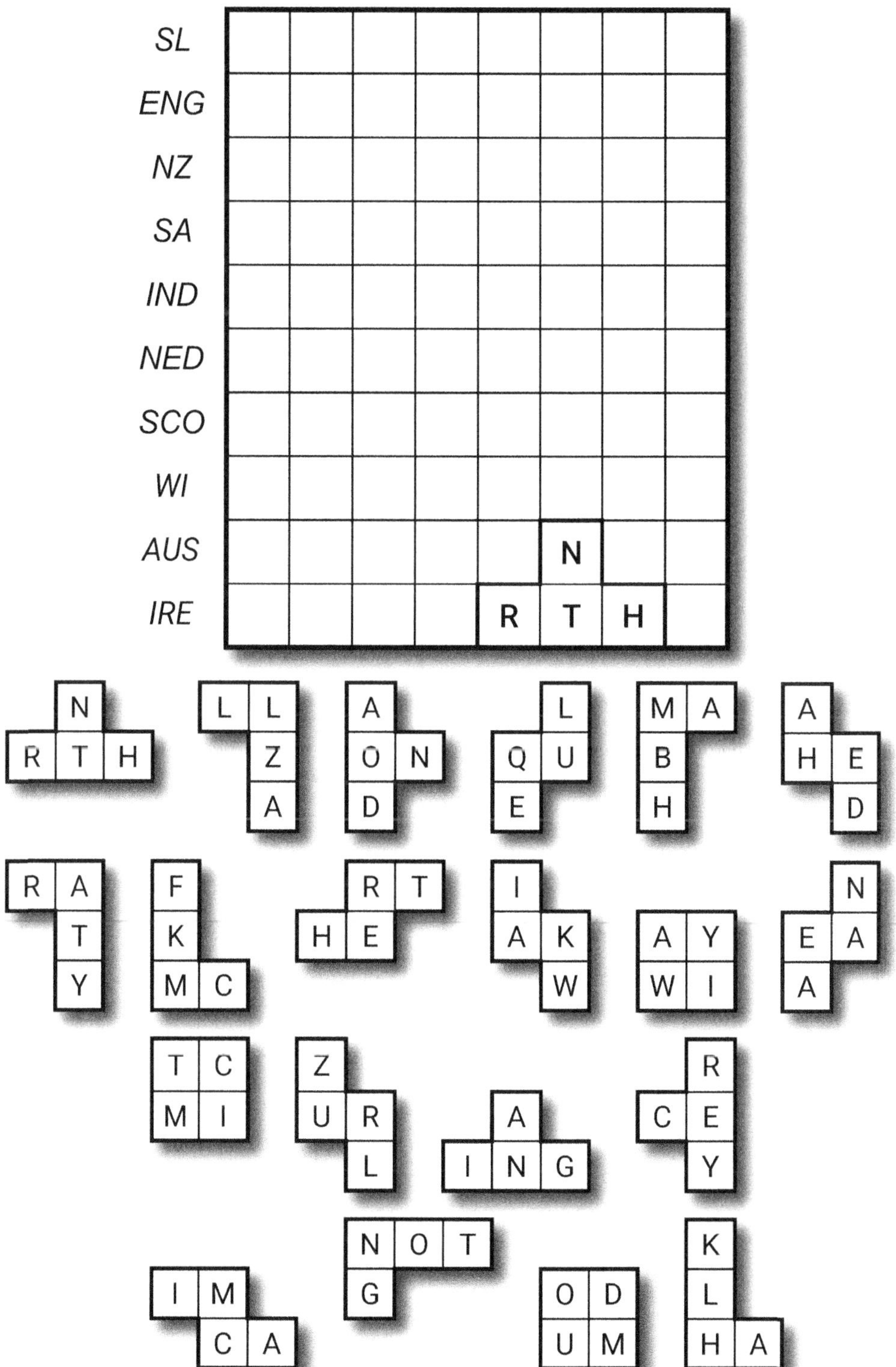

# WHO PLAYS WHO?



It's the Quarter-finals of the Global Qualifier for the ICC Cricket World Cup. From the information below can you work out who plays who?

"WE PLAY A TEAM WITH A LETTER **S** IN ITS NAME."

**BANGLADESH**

"OUR OPPONENT HAS A LETTER **T** IN ITS NAME."

**IRELAND**

"OUR OPPONENT HAS A LETTER **N** IN ITS NAME."

**NETHERLANDS**

"WE PLAY A TEAM WITH A LETTER **E** IN ITS NAME."

**UNITED ARAB EMIRATES**

"WE PLAY A TEAM WITH A LETTER **I** IN ITS NAME."

**ZIMBABWE**

"OUR OPPONENT HAS A LETTER **B** IN ITS NAME."

**SCOTLAND**

"OUR OPPONENT HAS A LETTER **H** IN ITS NAME."

**PAPUA NEW GUINEA**

"WE PLAY A TEAM WITH A LETTER **L** IN ITS NAME."

**THAILAND**

| QUARTER FINALS |
|---|
| v |
| v |
| v |
| v |

## CONNECTION 142

Can you sort the 16 past and present women's international cricketers into four connecting groups of 4 and identify what connects the groups. For example you might think that Carter, Hartenhof, Reilly and Taylor are members of the ICC Cricket Hall of Fame or have a surname that is also an occupation.

Note: Some cricketers may fall into more than one group but they only belong in one complete group of four.

| | | | |
|---|---|---|---|
| Shelley (AUS) **MOLINEUX** | Debbie (NZ) **FORD** | Nilakshi (SL) **SILVA** | Shauna (IRE) **MACMAHON** |
| Darcey (SCO) **CARTER** | Sarah (ENG) **ECCLESTONE** | Jolet (NED) **HARTENHOF** | Natasha (WI) **LEAN** |
| Mignon (SA) **PREEZ** | Lisa (AUS) **KEIGHTLEY** | Suzie (NZ) **DEVINE** | Mel (AUS) **JONES** |
| Stafanie (WI) **TAYLOR** | Lucy (IRE) **REILLY** | Yolani (SA) **FOURIE** | Georgia (ENG) **ADAMS** |

## PITCH IT UP 143

Enter the letters into their correct boxes in the vertical columns above to reveal the name of a women's international cricketer, their national team and four domestic teams they have played for around the cricket world.

| | | | | | | | | | | | | | | | |
|---|---|---|---|---|---|---|---|---|---|---|---|---|---|---|---|
| | | | | | | | | | | | | | | | |
| | | | | | | | | | | | | | | | |
| | | | | | | | | | | | | | | | S |
| | | | | | | | | | | | | | | | |
| | | | | | | | | | | | | | | | |
| | | | | | | | | | | | | | | | E |
| S | E | A | L | E | Y | N | T | S | N | O | B | E | L | E | ~~E~~ |
| W | Y | D | N | A | R | I | V | O | U | N | I | M | A | zZ | ~~S~~ |
| O | N | L | T | E | N | G | L | H | N | C | R | B | R | | |
| F | E | A | L | I | W | D | T | I | T | N | D | L | | | |
| W | R | G | N | | I | N | | S | O | | | | | | |
| E | V | S | L | | N | | | | | | | | | | |

# CROSS OVER 144

The answers in this puzzle are the 50 highest ranked women's T20I teams in the ICC's world rankings (at 20 October 2024). Can you complete the puzzle?

***3 LETTERS***

**PNG** (Papua New Guinea, East Asia-Pacific) *12th*
**UAE** (United Arab Emirates, Asia) *15th*
**USA** (United States of America, Americas) *27th*

***5 LETTERS***

**CHINA** (Asia) *48th*
**INDIA** (Asia) *3rd*
**ITALY** (Europe) *23rd*
**JAPAN** (Asia/East Asia-Pacific) *43rd*
**KENYA** (Africa) *28th*
**NEPAL** (Asia) *20th*
**SAMOA** (East Asia-Pacific) *50th*
**SPAIN** (Europe) *31st*

***6 LETTERS***

**BHUTAN** (Asia) *45th*
**BRAZIL** (Americas) *36th*
**CANADA** (Americas) *34th*

**CYPRUS** (Europe) *29th*
**FRANCE** (Europe) *35th*
**GREECE** (Europe) *39th*
**JERSEY** (Europe) *33rd*
**KUWAIT** (Asia) *49th*
**RWANDA** (Africa) *26th*
**SWEDEN** (Europe) *38th*
**UGANDA** (Africa) *18th*

*7 LETTERS*
**DENMARK** (Europe) *40th*
**ENGLAND** (Europe) *2nd*
**GERMANY** (Europe) *42nd*
**IRELAND** (Europe) *10th*
**MYANMAR** (Asia) *44th*
**NAMIBIA** (Africa) *17th*
**NIGERIA** (Africa) *24th*
**VANUATU** (East Asia-Pacific) *32nd*

*8 LETTERS*
**BOTSWANA** (Africa) *46th*
**GUERNSEY** (Europe) *41st*
**HONG KONG** (Asia) *22nd*
**MALAYSIA** (Asia) *27th*
**PAKISTAN** (Asia) *8th*
**SCOTLAND** (Europe) *11th*
**SRI LANKA** (Asia) *7th*
**TANZANIA** (Africa) *19th*
**THAILAND** (Asia) *13t*
**ZIMBABWE** (Africa) *14th*

*9 LETTERS*
**AUSTRALIA** (East Asia-Pacific) *1st*
**GIBRALTAR** (Europe) *30th*
**INDONESIA** (Asia/East Asia-Pacific) *21st*
**ISLE OF MAN** (Europe) *37th*

*10 LETTERS*
**BANGLADESH** (Asia) *9th*
**NEW ZEALAND** (East Asia-Pacific) *4th*
**WEST INDIES** (Americas) *6th*

*11 LETTERS*
**NETHERLANDS** (Europe) *16th*
**SIERRA LEONE** (Africa) *47th*
**SOUTH AFRICA** (Africa) *5th*

## STEPLADDER 145

Climb from **KARY** at the bottom of the ladder to **CHAN** at the top by changing just one letter to form a word and without disturbing the order of the remaining letters. The clues are provided to help you out but are not in the correct order.

KARY CHAN plays for Hong Kong Women (*64 WT20I's, 2019-24*).

| | |
|---|---|
| | CHAN |
| A tall cereal plant | |
| Inform of potential danger | |
| Not trusting someone completely | |
| Part of face below the mouth | |
| Invent a new word or expression | |
| Damaged or threadbare | |
| | KARY |

## MIDDLE ORDER 146

Arrange the letters found in **CHLOE ABEL** (SCO) (*11 WT20I's, 2023-24*) in the grid below to form six five-letter words reading across and down.

**C H L O E A B E L**

| | | | | |
|---|---|---|---|---|
| ■ | S | T | E | ■ |
| W | | | | E |
| R | | | | L |
| F | | | | K |
| ■ | L | O | T | ■ |

## SILHOUETTE 147

Can you name the women's international cricketer suggested by the images below?

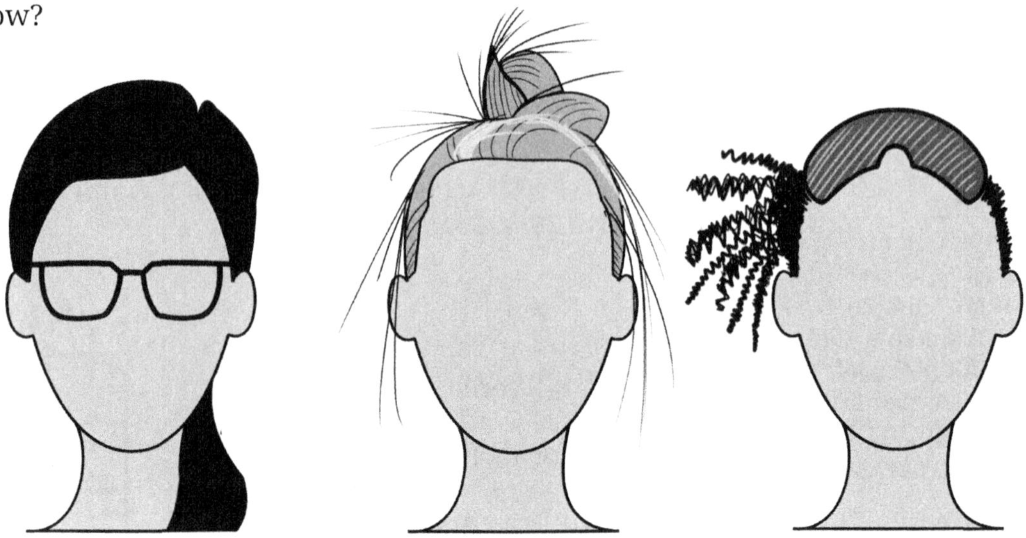

| PAKISTAN Women | ENGLAND Women | WEST INDIES Women |
|---|---|---|
| *77 WT20I's (2016-24)* | *164 WT20I's (2010-24)* | *160 WODI's (2008-24)* |

## BATTING ORDER 148

Can you rearrange the boxes of the grid below to spell the name of a women's international cricketer *(55 WODI's, 2013-22)*?

| | | |
|---|---|---|
| UR | LD | WI |
| HI | EN | LL |
| NF | LA | IE |

## DO YOU KNOW? 149

Which nations women's cricket team played a Test match seventeen years before its men's team played their first Test match?

A. NETHERLANDS
B. SRI LANKA
C. NEW ZEALAND
D. IRELAND
E. BANGLADESH

## CONUNDRUM 150

Can you unscramble the anagram to reveal the name of an India women's cricketer?

**A PHANTASY LIKER** (IND) (*16 WT20I's, 2023-24*)

## SQUARE CUT 151

Can you transfer the squares into the blank grid below so that a two-letter word is formed by each pair of adjoining letters and the name (6,6) of a Pakistan women's cricketer (*136 WODI's, 2006-24*) is spelt out reading anti-clockwise around the outside perimeter.

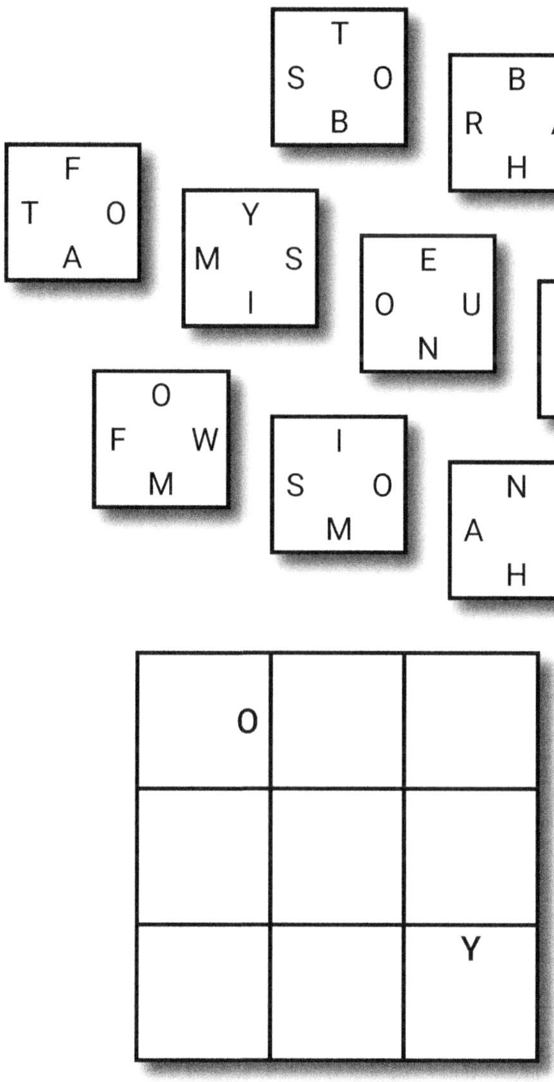


## MIXED UP PAIRS 152

Can you rearrange the pairs of letters to spell the name of an Australia women's cricketer *(20 WT20I's, 2018-24)*?

| EM | TA | CK | AV | IN | LA | YL |
|---|---|---|---|---|---|---|

## FIVEDOWN 153

Insert letters into the grid below to form five words reading across. When complete, the name of a Brazil women's cricketer (*15 WT20I's, 2022-24*) will be spelt out reading down the shaded squares.

| | | | | |
|---|---|---|---|---|
| A | | A | | S |
| P | | N | | C |
| D | | O | | L |
| S | | E | | E |
| C | | R | | T |

## MISSING LETTERS 154

Working from letter to adjacent letter in any direction can you spell out the name of an England women's cricketer (5,7) (*88 WODI's, 1999-2014*)?
You need to find the starting point and identify the missing letters.

| | | |
|---|---|---|
| A | B | ? |
| N | R | I |
| L | R | N |
| ? | D | A |

## ICC MEMBERS 155

The solutions to these seven clues are all ICC member countries and incorporate the letters found in the names of the women's international cricketers listed below. Each answer involves the addition of extra letters to name the ICC member. When complete, place one of the additional letters in the shaded box to reveal the name of another ICC member country.

MONI GRAY RANA TAAI ~~AMBO~~ NEED DONA

Capital city and ICC Region:

| Clue | | | | | | | | | | | | Shaded |
|---|---|---|---|---|---|---|---|---|---|---|---|---|
| 1. Phnom Penh, Asia | | A | M | B | O | | | | | | | |
| 2. Jakarta, East-Asia Pacific | | | | | | | | | | | | |
| 3. Dodoma, Africa | | | | | | | | | | | | |
| 4. Berlin, Europe | | | | | | | | | | | | |
| 5. Ulaanbaatar, Asia | | | | | | | | | | | | |
| 6. Amsterdam, Europe | | | | | | | | | | | | |
| 7. Colombo, Asia | | | | | | | | | | | | |

Name of ICC member: ..............................................

# 15 QUESTIONS WORDSEARCH



Can you find the answers to these quiz questions about women's international cricket hidden in the Wordsearch below? The answers can be found written across (forwards and backwards), up or down or diagonally?

| W | J | V | I | H | T | R | A | G | M | I | K | A | O | M | Z |
|---|---|---|---|---|---|---|---|---|---|---|---|---|---|---|---|
| E | O | D | W | R | I | L | D | H | A | R | D | L | T | I | N |
| J | S | R | E | M | E | P | A | N | C | N | Y | S | W | D | A |
| Z | E | G | L | S | U | Z | I | H | A | M | X | O | E | G | T |
| L | I | S | L | B | E | S | E | G | N | L | R | P | A | J | N |
| T | B | M | I | O | K | R | U | R | A | C | I | H | E | L | O |
| J | A | Q | N | A | N | E | T | H | E | R | L | A | N | D | S |
| E | S | Y | G | X | B | K | N | S | D | N | P | I | H | R | L |
| A | I | S | T | S | O | U | T | A | P | M | A | N | S | T | I |
| N | O | A | O | G | A | E | D | O | B | R | K | W | A | H | W |
| D | K | M | N | B | R | H | N | R | H | O | I | B | R | C | Y |
| U | F | A | J | I | D | C | U | A | L | Z | S | N | U | A | T |
| N | B | S | C | O | T | L | B | C | T | E | T | O | G | D | T |
| I | E | M | I | L | Y | D | R | U | M | M | A | L | T | S | E |
| H | N | U | B | N | A | C | G | O | D | U | N | I | H | A | B |
| R | O | M | A | H | T | L | A | E | W | N | O | M | M | O | C |

1. Which team's only appearance at a T20 Women's World Cup was in 2014?
2. What major Games, held every four years, included a women's cricket tournament for the first time in 2022?
3. Which women's national cricket team is known as the 'Green Shirts'?
4. Who captained New Zealand to success in the 2000 ICC Women's Cricket World Cup?
5. Which women's national cricket team is captained by Janet Mbabazi?
6. In which city was the final of the 2024 ICC Women's T20 World Cup held?
7. What is the nickname of West Indies women's cricketer Deandra Dottin?
8. Which women's team is the only current ICC Associate member to have played a Test match?
9. What is the name of the cricket ground in Almeria, Spain that has played host to numerous women's T20I matches?
10. In 1958, who became the first cricketer, male or female, to take 10 wickets and score a century in a Test match?
11. Which current Australia women's cricketer has also played international cricket for Ireland?
12. What animal features on the logo/badge of the Bangladesh women's cricket team?
13. Which cathedral city, located in England, has hosted the most number of women's Test matches?
14. In addition to Sri Lanka, for which other nation has Deepika Rasangika also played international cricket?
15. Amanda-Jade .........., Australia women's cricketer who has the same surname as the capital city of an ICC Full member nation?

## SIDE ON 157

Can you pair the following words and transfer them into the list below to spell the names of 10 women's international cricketers?

SON ARM GOOD SOLE ARE WARE TIN

WAR CHIP DOT SWEET ALL CAR

MAN SHRUB ROOF HAM MA TAN STRONG

| | |
|---|---|
| Anya ........................................ | ENG, *86 WODI's, 2008-22* |
| Bismah ........................................ | PAK, *136 WODI's 2006-24* |
| Eden ........................................ | NZ, *31 WT20I's, 2022-24* |
| Georgia ........................................ | AUS, *63 WT20I's, 2018-24* |
| Neha ........................................ | IND, *5 WODI's, 2011* |
| Deandra ........................................ | WI, *143 WODI's, 2008-22* |
| Donna ........................................ | IRE, *20 WODI's, 1987-91* |
| Francisca ........................................ | ZIM, *16 WT20I's, 2022-24* |
| Caroline ........................................ | SCO, *4 WODIs, 2001-03* |
| Lara ........................................ | SA, *50 WODI's, 2016-24* |

---

## SCORECARD 158

Nepal Women are batting first in a fantasy WT20I match against Malaysia Women at the Tribhuvan University International Cricket Ground, Kirtipur, Nepal. Can you crack the logical code behind the runs scored and work out how many runs Puja Mahato and Kabita Joshi score?

| NEPAL Women | | |
|---|---|---|
| Kabita Kunwar | c Wan Julia b Winifred Duraisingham | 22 |
| Sita Rana Magar | lbw b Mahirah Izzati Ismail | 50 |
| Indu Barma (c) | b Winifred Duraisingham | 11 |
| Rubina Chhetry | b Ainna Hamizah Hashim | 21 |
| Dolly Bhatta | st Wan Julia b Nur Dania Syuhada | 6 |
| Puja Mahato | lbw b Aisya Eleesa | ? |
| Kabita Joshi (wk) | c Mas Elysa b Mahirah Izzati Ismail | ? |

## CRIDOKU 159

Fill in the squares of the grid so that each row, each column and each smaller 3x3 block contains all the letters which spell **JOS BURLEY** (NZ) (*6 WTests, 1966-69*) only once.

| | | | | | | | | |
|---|---|---|---|---|---|---|---|---|
| O | B | | | | | | J | Y |
| Y | | | | | | | | R |
| | | L | | U | | E | | |
| L | | | O | | U | | | B |
| | | Y | | B | | R | | |
| B | | | R | | L | | | E |
| | | B | | R | | Y | | |
| J | | | | | | | | S |
| U | E | | | | | | R | J |

## INSIDE OUT 160

Enter a word in the spaces of each row to spell a seven letter word. When complete the shaded squares will spell out the surname of a Thailand women's cricketer (*88 WT20I's, 2018-24*).

| | | | | | | |
|---|---|---|---|---|---|---|
| E | X | | | | L | Y |
| A | N | T | | | | S |
| S | | | | L | T | H |
| C | A | | | | E | T |
| P | | | | E | S | S |
| L | O | | | | E | D |
| A | D | M | | | | R |

## CRICKET UMPIRES 161

Can you match the female cricket umpires to the correct nationality?

| | |
|---|---|
| Eloise Sheridan | West Indies |
| Nimali Perera | New Zealand |
| Sue Redfern | India |
| Jacqueline Williams | Sri Lanka |
| Sarah Dambanevana | Australia |
| Kathy Cross | England |
| Vrinda Rathi | Zimbabwe |

# CRICKET JUMBO CODEWORD



Each number in the grid represents a different letter of the alphabet. Can you complete the grid correctly and also identify the surnames of 10 England women's cricketers hidden in the squares?

| | | | | | | | | | | | | |
|---|---|---|---|---|---|---|---|---|---|---|---|---|
| 1 | 11 | 14 | 4 | 23 | | 5 | 12 | 26 | 24 | 16 | 4 | 23 |
| | 8 | | 7 | | 25 | | 26 | | 19 | | 13 | |
| 21 | 11 | 5 | 5 | 4 | 23 | | 24 | 18 | 10 | 10 | 4 | 16 |
| | 24 | | 23 | | 11 | | 5 | | 12 | | 24 | |
| 12 | 4 | 23 | 11 | 19 | 17 | 9 | | 17 | 5 | 11 | 19 | 25 |
| | | | 13 | | 17 | | 17 | | 25 | | 24 | |
| 18 | 25 | 12 | 4 | 16 | | 18 | 21 | 11 | 3 | 11 | 10 | 15 |
| | 11 | | 23 | | 18 | | 3 | | 26 | | | |
| 2 | 26 | 19 | 5 | | 17 | 24 | 11 | 20 | 6 | 18 | 3 | 3 |
| | 23 | | | | 17 | | 16 | | | | 19 | |
| 17 | 5 | 18 | 23 | 3 | 19 | 24 | 10 | | 25 | 18 | 14 | 4 |
| | | | 4 | | 10 | | 4 | | 4 | | 4 | |
| 16 | 4 | 18 | 22 | 4 | 24 | 17 | | 9 | 18 | 23 | 17 | 12 |
| | 15 | | 26 | | 17 | | 6 | | 17 | | | |
| 12 | 4 | 18 | 5 | 12 | | 1 | 26 | 14 | 4 | 6 | 11 | 7 |
| | 17 | | 18 | | 6 | | 3 | | 22 | | 5 | |
| 17 | 11 | 9 | 6 | 23 | 4 | | 14 | 24 | 19 | 10 | 12 | 5 |
| | 23 | | 3 | | 3 | | 15 | | 23 | | 4 | |
| 23 | 4 | 13 | 4 | 18 | 3 | 17 | | 20 | 4 | 19 | 23 | 16 |

A B C D E F G H I J K L M N O P Q R S T U V W X Y Z

| | | | | | | | | | | | | |
|---|---|---|---|---|---|---|---|---|---|---|---|---|
| 1 | 2 | 3 | 4 | 5 | 6 | 7 | 8 | 9 | 10 | 11 | 12 | 13 |
| 14 | 15 Y | 16 | 17 | 18 | 19 | 20 | 21 | 22 F | 23 | 24 | 25 | 26 |

# ICC ODI CRICKETER OF THE YEAR 163

From only the vowels in their names (and with consonants removed) can you identify the winners of the ICC Women's ODI Cricketer of the Year Award since it was introduced in 2012.

| Year | Clue | Answer |
|---|---|---|
| 2012 & 14 | **AAIE AO** (WI) | ........................ |
| 2013 & 16 | **UIE AE** (NZ) | ........................ |
| 2015 | **E AI** (AUS) | ........................ |
| 2017 | **A AEAIE** (NZ) | ........................ |
| 2018 | **II AAA** (IND) | ........................ |
| 2019 | **EE E** (AUS) | ........................ |
| 2021 | **IEE EE** (SA) | ........................ |
| 2022 | **A IE-U** (ENG) | ........................ |
| 2023 | **AAI AAAU** (SL) | ........................ |

## CRICKET CIRCLES 164

Replace the question marks with letters so that the letters in each circle can be arranged to spell the surnames of three women cricketers who all play for the same national team. Can you name the cricketers and the team?

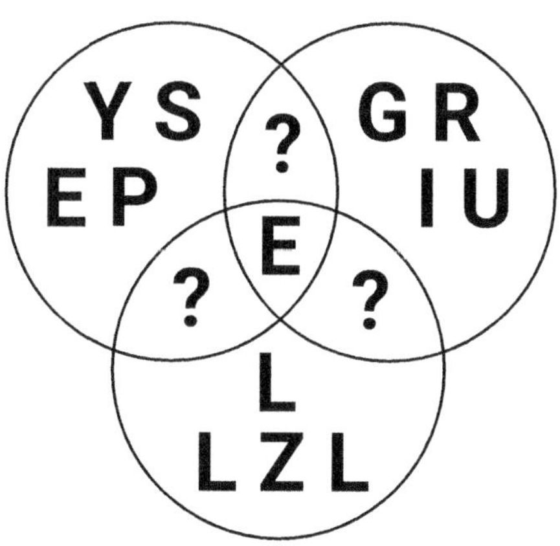


## HIT FOR SIX 165

Complete the grid so that every row and column, and every outlined area, contains each of the letters found in the surname of Katey **MARTIN** (NZ) (*103 WODI's, 2003-22*).

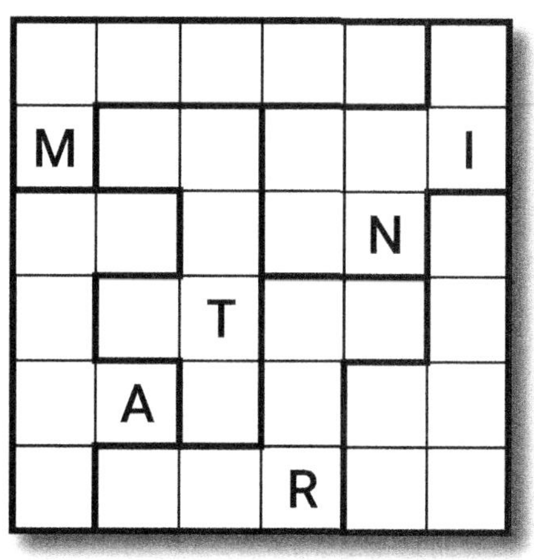

# FOLLOW ON



Every answer to each clue (except the first) starts with the last letter of the preceding answer, and when entered into the grid follows a spiral path reading anti-clockwise to the centre. When complete, the shaded diagonal squares will spell out the name of a women's international cricketer and a domestic team they have played for.

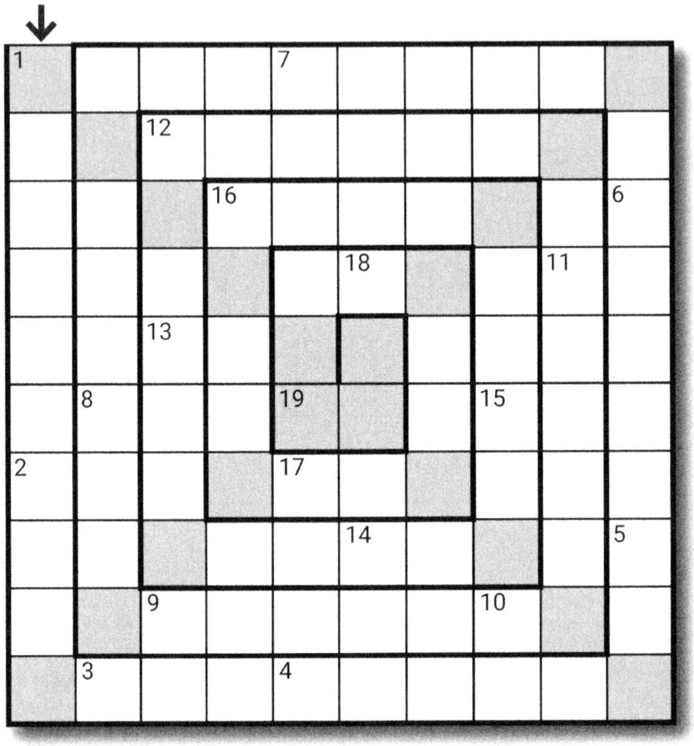


1. Argue or make objections about a trivial matter (7)
2. A small digital pictogram used in electronic messages, eg. texts, emails (5)
3. Skin irritation causing a desire to scratch (4)
4. The science of armorial insignia, including shields, crests, symbols, etc (8)
5. Semi-fluid food produced by the bacterial fermentation of milk (6)
6. A young person whose age is between 13-19 years old (8)
7. Displaying extreme pleasure, happiness or excitement (9)
8. To decide against doing something which was planned (5)
9. A government department; a writing desk with drawers (6)
10. Not easy to see, hear or understand (7)
11. A course, usually oval, on which runners, horses, cars, etc compete (9)
12. Large, brown plant that grows in the sea, used for food and medicine (4)
13. Make something last longer (7)
14. Large, ambitious, or impressive in scale (5)
15. To reduce in size, importance or value (8)
16. Full of activity, or very busy and fast-paced (6)
17. A pipe carrying waste water under roads, railways, etc (7)
18. Large saltwater fish, caught extensively for food (4)
19. Small, poisonous snake, found espec. in S. Europe and N. Africa (3)

# NATIONALITY? 167

Listed below are the highest individual scores for each batting position in women's T20I matches. However, the nation that each player represents is missing. Can you complete the list by correctly placing the following teams against the relevant cricketer in the grid?

NAMIBIA SRI LANKA JERSEY UGANDA SAMOA
ARGENTINA INDIA WEST INDIES NEPAL AUSTRIA

| POS. | PLAYER | RUNS | TEAM | OPPOSITION | YEAR |
|---|---|---|---|---|---|
| Open. | Lucia Taylor | 169 | | Chile | 2023 |
| 3 | Deepika Rasangika | 161* | | Saudi Arabia | 2022 |
| 4 | Rubina Chhetry | 118* | | Maldives | 2024 |
| 5 | Harmanpreet Kaur | 103 | | New Zealand | 2018 |
| 6 | Deandra Dottin | 112* | | South Africa | 2010 |
| 7 | Rita Musamali | 55* | | Malawi | 2024 |
| 8 | Grace Wetherall | 57* | | Germany | 2023 |
| 9 | Andrea-Mae Zepeda | 49* | | Czech Rep. | 2024 |
| 10 | Anneri van Schoor | 39* | | Botswana | 2019 |
| 11 | Florence Agaimalo | 21* | | Vanuatu | 2022 |

# PAIR UP 168

The 4-letter surnames of seven India women's cricketers are jumbled up in the grid below. Can you match the pair of letters and work out which pair is not used?

| AR | NA | IN | MA | SI |
|---|---|---|---|---|
| LA | DH | KA | IK | DE |
| UT | JA | NI | OL | RA |

## STAIRCASE 169

Arrange the surnames of the seven West Indies women's cricketers listed below so that when placed in the horizontal rows of the grid, the letters of the diagonal 'staircase' spell out an eighth cricketer (WI, *47 WT20I's, 2019-24*).

DALEY GLASGOW MUNROE ATKINS GREGG ETIENNE LEWIS

## MID-OFF 170

Can you identify the Pakistan women's cricketer (*37 WT20I's, 2016-23*) whose surname fits in the sequence of words below?

**RAN**
**NEAR**
**?????**
**WARNED**
**PREDAWN**

## VARIATION 171

Can you complete the grid so that every row and column contain each of the letters found in the surname of Sobhana **MOSTARY** (BAN) (*42 WT20I's, 2019-24*)?

| | | | | | | |
|---|---|---|---|---|---|---|
| R | | | | | Y | |
| | M | | | S | | O |
| | A | | | T | | |
| Y | | | S | | | |
| | | T | | | S | |
| A | | | Y | | R | |
| | | | | M | | |

## MATCH UP

172

Can you transfer the following suffixes and nations to the list below to complete the names of five women's cricket teams and where they are based?

**HEARTS** **PHOENIX** **HEAT**

**CAPITALS** **PROVINCE** **~~AMAZON WARRIORS~~**

*South Africa* *Australia* *~~West Indies~~* *New Zealand* *India* *England*

| | | |
|---|---|---|
| GUYANA | **AMAZON WARRIORS** | *West Indies* |
| BIRMINGHAM | ............................................................ | .......................... |
| BRISBANE | ............................................................ | .......................... |
| DELHI | ............................................................ | .......................... |
| WESTERN | ............................................................ | .......................... |
| AUCKLAND | ............................................................ | .......................... |

---

## PATHFINDER

173

Starting from the shaded letter, move up, down or sideways (but NOT diagonally) to find a route through the grid that spells out the 9 countries beginning with the letter 'B' that are members of the ICC. The route should form a continuous line through each of the letters in the grid, ending back at the shaded square.

Note: The name of a country that is not an ICC member has also been included in the grid. Can you spot it?

| | | | | | | | | |
|---|---|---|---|---|---|---|---|---|
| E | R | M | S | W | A | L | I | Z |
| B | N | U | T | O | N | E | B | E |
| A | I | D | A | B | A | B | A | N |
| R | B | M | U | L | U | E | D | G |
| H | A | G | I | G | **B** | S | A | L |
| B | E | L | R | A | N | H | B | E |
| L | A | R | I | T | A | S | U | L |
| I | Z | B | A | U | H | B | R | A |

## OUTSIDE EDGE **174**

Can you divide the following words into two and transfer the letters into the grid below to spell the surnames of 10 women's international cricketers? Note, the divided letters can be placed either at the start or end of the cricketer's name.

| | | | | |
|---|---|---|---|---|
| ~~ROGUES~~ | POSH | BERTH | HOARD | LAVA |
| CELL | SENDER | MOOD | SASH | MANGO |

LIST OF CRICKETERS

| | | | |
|---|---|---|---|
| RO | **DRI** | GUES | *IND, 104 WT20I's, 2018-24* |
| | **CK** | | *SA, 19 WT20I's, 2023-24* |
| | **AQS** | | *SCO, 57 WT20I's, 2018-24* |
| | **IHE** | | *NAM, 66 WT20I's, 2018-24* |
| | **TI** | | *UAE, 75 WT20I's, 2021-24* |
| | **ER** | | *IRE, 15 WODI's, 2002-09* |
| | **W** | | *NED, 21 WODI's, 1990-99* |
| | **GHE** | | *USA, 23 WT20I's, 2021-24* |
| | **ONN** | | *WI, 77 WT20I's, 2014-24* |
| | **DLI** | | *ENG, 11 WODI's, 2002-03* |

## CRICKET (DING)BATS **175**

Can you identify the cricket-related terms suggested by the images below?

1. ..................................................

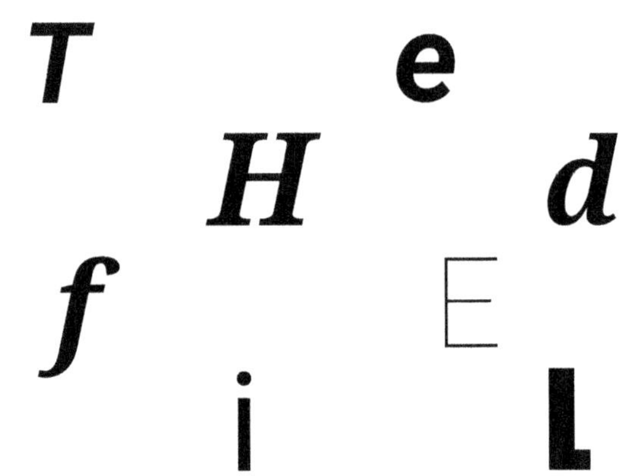


2. ..................................................

# LOGIC PUZZLE



South Africa's Laura Wolvaardt has had an eventful innings in a fantasy WODI against New Zealand Women. From the information below can you match the incident that occurred off which bowler, the shot Laura was playing and how may runs she'd scored?

**Clues:**

1. Laura had made more than 50 runs before facing the bowling of Lea Tahuhu.
2. With her score on an even number of runs Laura needed medical treatment after being hit on the thumb when attempting a reverse sweep.
3. Laura was in double figures when accidently running out Sune Luus calling for a quick single off the bowling of Fran Jonas. She hadn't just played a leg glance.
4. The incident off the bowling of Amelia Kerr involved a straight hit; Laura had made 27 runs at the time of playing the square cut.
5. The review for LBW came before the incident off the bowling of Rosemary Mair - which was not the shot of the day that took Laura to 110.
6. Laura wasn't on 73 runs when Izzy Gaze dropped a difficult chance; but she was on 58 runs when the incident occurred off the bowling of Hannah Rowe.

| | Fran Jonas | Amelia Kerr | Rosemary Mair | Hannah Rowe | Lea Tahuhu | Cover drive | Leg glance | Reverse sweep | Square cut | Straight hit | 9 | 27 | 58 | 73 | 106 |
|---|---|---|---|---|---|---|---|---|---|---|---|---|---|---|---|
| Dropped catch | | | | | | | | | | | | | | | |
| LBW review | | | | | | | | | | | | | | | |
| Medical treatment | | | | | | | | | | | | | | | |
| Run out partner | | | | | | | | | | | | | | | |
| Shot of the day | | | | | | | | | | | | | | | |
| 9 | | | | | | | | | | | | | | | |
| 27 | | | | | | | | | | | | | | | |
| 58 | | | | | | | | | | | | | | | |
| 73 | | | | | | | | | | | | | | | |
| 106 | | | | | | | | | | | | | | | |
| Cover drive | | | | | | | | | | | | | | | |
| Leg glance | | | | | | | | | | | | | | | |
| Reverse sweep | | | | | | | | | | | | | | | |
| Square cut | | | | | | | | | | | | | | | |
| Straight hit | | | | | | | | | | | | | | | |

Tip: Use the grid to record all the positive or negative facts obtained from the clues. By placing a tick or cross in the relevant squares of the grid, and cross-referencing the clues, you will be able to work out all the correct facts.

| RUNS SCORED | BOWLER | INCIDENT | SHOT PLAYED |
|---|---|---|---|
| | | | |
| | | | |
| | | | |
| | | | |
| | | | |

## BATTING ORDER 177

Can you rearrange the boxes of the grid below to spell the name of a women's international cricketer *(64 WODI's, 2014-22)*?

| | | |
|---|---|---|
| WA | JE | YA |
| AD | KW | RI |
| RA | SH | GA |

## SIX DOWN 178

Insert letters into the grid below to form six words reading across. When complete, the name of a Vanuatu women's cricketer (*40 WT20I's, 2019-24*) will be spelt out reading down the shaded squares.

| | | | | |
|---|---|---|---|---|
| B | | E | | D |
| H | | U | | T |
| A | | I | | S |
| S | | A | | E |
| F | | V | | R |
| C | | O | | N |

## CROSSWORD 4s 179

Can you complete the puzzle by correctly placing the four-letter cricket-related words into the crossword?

ROPE HELD TOSS OVER RISK POST LEAD PAIR SAFE LOOP
TAIL DUCK AREA HEAD TIED LOSS DIVE TAKE LATE DASH

## ROTATION 180

Find the starting point and fill in the blanks to reveal the name (6,10) of an England women's cricketer (*90 WT20I's, 2016-24*). Only alternate letters are shown.

## INSIDE OUT 181

Enter a word in the spaces of each row to spell a seven letter word. When complete the shaded squares will spell out the surname of a New Zealand women's cricketer (*52 WODI's, 2010-16*).

| U | N | K | ■ |   |   | N |
|---|---|---|---|---|---|---|
| M | A |   | ■ |   | E | E |
| B | E | N | ■ |   |   | H |
| V |   |   | ■ | A | G | E |
| R | A | N | ■ |   |   | K |
| G | E |   | ■ |   | I | C |
| A |   |   | ■ | D | O | N |

## PITCH IT UP 182

Enter the letters into their correct boxes in the vertical columns above to reveal the name of a women's international cricketer, their national team and four domestic teams they have played for around the cricket world.

|   |   |   |   |   | ■ |   |   |   |   |   | ■ | ■ | ■ | ■ |
|---|---|---|---|---|---|---|---|---|---|---|---|---|---|---|
|   |   |   |   |   | ■ |   |   |   |   |   |   | ■ | ■ | ■ |
|   |   |   |   |   |   |   | ■ |   |   |   |   |   |   | S |
|   |   |   |   |   |   | ■ |   |   |   |   |   |   | ■ | ■ |
|   |   |   |   |   |   |   | ■ |   |   |   |   |   |   | G |
|   |   |   |   |   |   | ■ |   |   |   |   |   |   |   | ■ |

| M | H | U | T | R | D | A | S | G | U | O | R | N | S | ~~S~~ |
|---|---|---|---|---|---|---|---|---|---|---|---|---|---|---|
| S | U | N | B | A | Y | O | F | N | X | I | A | E | L | ~~G~~ |
| C | Y | M | O | H | I | T | R | I | R | E | Y | A | N |   |
| S | A | D | T | E | A | L | S | Y | I | N | A | S |   |   |
| B | O | R | N | A |   |   | I | R | O | C | T |   |   |   |
| C | E | L | B | E |   |   |   |   | D | A |   |   |   |   |

# SUPER CRICTETRIS



Drop each of the shapes from the top of the grid to spell the surnames of ten women's international cricketers reading across. One of the shapes has been dropped to help you get started.
Note: The shapes should not be rotated or reflected and must be able to be dropped into the grid so that they come to rest on another shape or grid bottom.

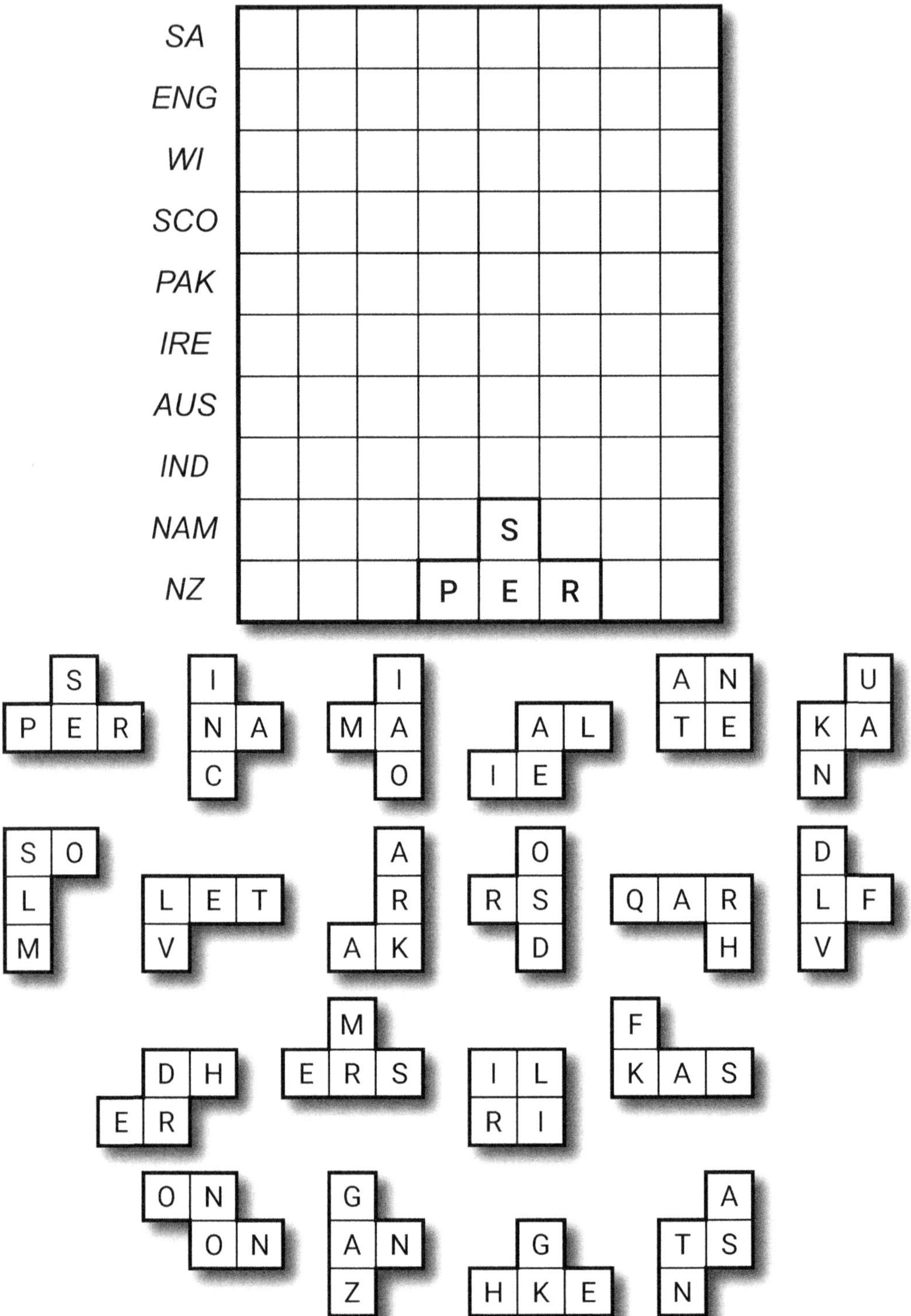

## BRAINTEASER 184

A T20 international match has just finished between Sri Lanka Women and Netherlands Women.

Batting first, Sri Lanka scored 146 for 4. In the run chase Netherlands scored at a rate of 5.75 in their first 12 overs and 9.50 runs off the remaining 8 overs, losing 7 wickets.

Who won the match?

## MIDDLE ORDER 185

Arrange the letters found in **EVE CAESAR** (WI) (*6 WODI's, 1993*) in the grid below to form six five-letter words reading across and down.

**EVE CAESAR**

| | | | | |
|---|---|---|---|---|
| ■ | B | N | O | ■ |
| L | | | | E |
| R | | | | T |
| S | | | | F |
| ■ | H | L | S | ■ |

## BUMP BALL 186

Can you identify the missing letters that complete the surnames of 6 Australia women cricketers?
Next, rearrange the missing letters to spell the surname of another Australia women's cricketer (*19 WODI's, 2008-10*).

| | | | | | |
|---|---|---|---|---|---|
| H | A | | N | E | S |
| S | T | R | | N | O |
| R | | E | L | E | R |
| J | A | C | O | | S |
| | C | H | U | T | T |
| C | O | O | P | E | |

## MIXED UP THREE'S 187

Can you rearrange the groups of letters to spell the name of an international women's cricketer *(90 WT20I's, 2018-24)*?

| | | | | | | |
|---|---|---|---|---|---|---|
| KAI | NAN | OEN | HAR | ONC | ATK | NAP |

# CROSS OVER 188

The answers in this puzzle are the 44 women's international cricketers who have scored a century in WT20I's. Can you complete the puzzle?

Note: Where a player has recorded more than one WT20I century there highest score is indicated in the list below.

*3 LETTERS*
MUNEEBA **ALI** (PAK) *102*
**LEE** Lizelle (IRE) *101*
**OZA** Esha (UAE) *158**

*4 LETTERS*
**ABEL** Queentor (KEN) *109*
**HILL** Mariko (HK) *100**
**KAUR** Harmanpreet (IND) *103*

*5 LETTERS*
**ALAKO** Prosscovia (UGA) *116*
**AYSHA** (QTR) *113**
**BATES** Suzie (NZ) *124**
**BLAKE** Rebecca (ROU) *135**
**FRITZ** Shandre (SA) *116**
**GALAN** Albertina (ARG) *145**
**GOUGH** Christina (GER) *101**
**HEALY** Alyssa (AUS) *148**
Fargana **HOQUE** (BAN) *110**
**KALIS** Sterre (NL) *126**
**LEWIS** Gaby (IRE) *119*
**WYATT** - HODGE Danni (ENG) *124*

*6 LETTERS*
**AGATHA** Laura (BRA) *144**
**ANDREW** Rachel (VAN) *106**
**DEVINE** Sophie (NZ) *105*
**DOTTIN** Deandra (WI) *112**
**HUNTER** Amy (IRE) *101**

**KIBASU** Fatuma (TAN) *127**
**KNIGHT** Heather (ENG) *108**
**MOONEY** Beth (AUS) *117**
**TAYLOR** Lucia (ARG) *169*
**ZEPEDA** Andrea-Mae (AUT) *101*

*7 LETTERS*
**BAHADUR** Shahreen (QAT) *104**
**CHHETRY** Rubina (NEP) *118**
**ISHIMWE** Gisele (RWA) *114**
**LANNING** Meg (AUS) *133**
NIGAR **SULTANA** (BAN) *113**
**RONALDS** Janet (GER) *105**
**VASQUEZ** Veronica (ARG) *107**

*8 LETTERS*
**BEAUMONT** Tammy (ENG) *116*
**MATTHEWS** Hayley (WI) *132*
**MUSAMALI** Rita (UGA) *103**

*9 LETTERS*
**ANGGRAENI** Yulia (IDN) *112*
**RASANGIKA** Deepika (BAH) *161**
**WOLVAARDT** Laura (SA) *102*

*11 LETTERS*
**ATHAPATHTHU** Chamari (SL) *119**
**BIMENYIMANA** Marie (RWA) *114**
**CASTINEIRAS** Maria (ARG) *155**

## STEPLADDER 189

Climb from **SIAN** at the bottom of the ladder to **RUCK** at the top by changing just one letter to form a word and without disturbing the order of the remaining letters. The clues are provided to help you out but are not in the correct order.

SIAN RUCK is a former cricketer for New Zealand Women (*37 WT20I's, 2009-13*).

| Clue | Ladder |
|---|---|
| | RUCK |
| Exchange one thing for another | |
| Substance used for washing | |
| Item of clothing; hit with force | |
| Solid part of the earth's surface | |
| Large waterbird with long neck | |
| To leave in liquid, eg. to clean | |
| | SIAN |

## FOURS 190

Can you identify the Australia women's cricketer (*8 WTests, 1961-72*) whose surname can be placed before HIGH, CAP, JOINT and DEEP to make two new words or phrases?

HIGH
CAP
JOINT
DEEP

## MISSING LETTERS 191

Working from letter to adjacent letter in any direction can you spell out the name of an Australia women's cricketer (6,6) (*50 WODI's, 2014-19*). You need to find the starting point and identify the missing letters.

| | | |
|---|---|---|
| ? | O | N |
| O | L | O |
| C | L | B |
| N | I | ? |

## CRIDOKU 192

Fill in the squares of the grid so that each row, each column and each smaller 3x3 block contains all the letters which spell **AMY HUNTER** (IRE) (*40 WT20I's, 2021-24*) only once.

| | | | | | | | | |
|---|---|---|---|---|---|---|---|---|
| | Y | | | | E | | | |
| | | | H | | A | E | | T |
| | | T | | | | Y | | M |
| | | | | | H | M | | U |
| H | | | E | | M | | | A |
| A | | Y | N | | | | | |
| R | | M | | | | U | | |
| N | | E | T | | R | | | |
| | | | U | | | | T | |

## HIT FOR SIX 193

Complete the grid so that every row and column, and every outlined area, contains each of the letters found in the surname of Shikha **PANDEY** (IND) (*55 WODI's, 2014-21*).

| | | | | | |
|---|---|---|---|---|---|
| | N | | | E | |
| | | | | | |
| | | Y | | P | |
| A | | | | | |
| | | | D | | |
| | | | | | |

## RECORD HOLDER 194

One of the longest-standing records in Women's ODI's is held by Gill Smith (ENG, *1986-93*).

Gill, who played 31 WODI's for England between 1986-93, took 41 wickets and holds the record for the lowest career bowling average*.

What was Gill's average?

A. 10.47
B. 12.53
C. 15.61
D. 18.79

* Minimum 1,000 balls bowled

# CRICKET CROSSWORD 195

ACROSS

1. Wellington .........., women's cricket team that competes in New Zealand's HBJ Shield and Women's Super Smash (5)
4. Format in which cricket teams play each other to determine a winner (6)
8. Jahanara .........., Bangladesh medium-pace bowler (*80 WT20I's, 2012-24*) (4)
9. National cricket team captained by Kary Chan (4,4)
10. Period of continuous bowling by a player (5)
12. Action of batter moving quickly towards the bowling delivery for a powerful hit (6)
15. See 3 down (3)
17. Richa .........., India wicket-keeper batter (*59 WT20I's, 2020-24*) (5)
18. Muneeba .........., Pakistan wicket-keeper batter (*77 WT20I's, 2016-24*) (3)
19. Capricorn .........., nickname of Namibia women's national cricket team (6)
21. The ability to play cricket well (5)
25. A bowler must not do this - in relation to the popping crease (8)
26. .......... Park, sports stadium and cricket venue in Auckland, New Zealand (4)
27. Hasini .........., Sri Lanka middle-order batter (*84 WT20I's, 2014-24*) (6)
28. .......... Sultana Joty, Bangladesh wicket-keeper batter and captain (*103 WT20I's, 2015-24*) (5)

DOWN

2. Action of batter not attempting to play the ball (5)
3. and 15 across: UAE all-rounder and captain of national team (*88 WT20I's, 2018-24*) (4)
4. The first of two intervals during a full day's play (5)
5. .......... Elwiss, Southern Vipers and England medium-pace bowler (*36 WODI's, 2011-19*) (7)
6. Also known as a snick or nick off the bat (4)
7. Abtaha .........., Scotland leg-spin bowler (*57 WT20I's, 2018-24*) (7)
11. A bowling delivery that is not a no-ball (5)
12. .......... bat shot, a shot played with the bat parallel with the ground, eg. a cut or pull (5)
13. International cricket series between England and Australia (5)
14. Elyse .........., Tasmania and Australia top-order batter (*62 WT20I's, 2009-18*) (7)
16. A non-professional cricketer (7)
20. A run awarded to the batting team that is not credited to a batter (5)
22. Nation scheduled to host the 2025 ICC Women's Cricket World Cup (5)
23. Curved path of ball delivered by spinner (4)
24. To bat first or start an innings (4)

# WORDSEARCH



The surnames of the 20 cricketers who have played the most WT20I's for Zimbabwe Women have been hidden in the Wordsearch below. Their names can be found horizontally (forwards and backwards), vertically (up or down) or diagonally. Can you find all 20 players?

| | | | | | | | | | | | | | | | |
|---|---|---|---|---|---|---|---|---|---|---|---|---|---|---|---|
| S | H | W | I | M | A | B | H | E | R | O | M | L | E | S | M |
| A | M | U | H | S | T | W | N | C | Y | E | U | A | I | U | A |
| N | M | R | E | N | O | M | K | H | T | R | G | B | S | E | R |
| D | C | U | W | D | H | U | O | I | S | U | A | N | M | Z | N |
| H | O | H | G | I | M | J | M | U | H | N | I | U | A | H | D |
| L | I | D | N | E | W | A | O | S | D | C | T | Y | B | R | I |
| O | G | R | A | P | R | J | T | A | V | Z | A | M | H | Q | G |
| V | T | X | H | O | A | I | M | R | M | H | N | P | E | T | C |
| U | J | I | S | K | M | U | T | A | S | A | U | S | U | G | H |
| P | R | L | U | N | K | B | E | I | W | H | R | P | W | M | I |
| I | N | U | M | O | I | D | V | G | R | E | S | A | I | H | P |
| H | T | A | R | S | M | Z | R | M | Y | I | N | T | N | K | A |
| C | W | J | V | U | A | F | S | A | H | Z | P | U | M | G | R |
| G | U | N | Z | M | H | T | M | D | U | L | O | A | B | V | E |
| M | A | Y | A | R | I | D | N | R | T | K | G | I | N | A | D |
| D | B | O | M | U | N | S | A | D | N | O | S | U | M | O | M |

Number of WT20I appearances at 20 October 2024:

**CHIPARE** Francisca (ZIM, *2022-24*) *16*
**DHURURU** Chiedza (ZIM, *2019-24*) *37*
**GRANGER** Tasmeen (ZIM, *2019-21*) *14*
**GWANZURA** Nyasha (ZIM, *2021-24*) *17*
**MABHERO** Lindokuhle (ZIM, *2023-24*) *16*
**MARANGE** Precious (ZIM, *2019-24*) *60*
**MAYERS** Sharne (ZIM, *2019-24*) *33*
**MAZVISHAYA** Audrey (ZIM, *2019-24*) *25*
**MUGERI-TIRIPANO** Chipo (ZIM, *2019-24*) *54*
**MUJAJI** Pellagia (ZIM, *2021-24*) *28*
**MUPACHIKWA** Modester (ZIM, *2019-24*) *59*
**MUSHANGWE** Anesu (ZIM, *2019-22*) *21*
**MUSONDA** Mary-Anne (ZIM, *2019-24*) *58*
**MUTASA** Nomatter (ZIM, *2019-21*) *11*
**NDHLOVU** Kelis (ZIM, *2022-24*) *45*
**NDIRAYA** Ashley (ZIM, *2019-24*) *29*
**NKOMO** Josephine (ZIM, *2019-24*) *57*
**PHIRI** Loryn (ZIM, *2019-24*) *32*
**SIBANDA** Nomvelo (ZIM, *2019-24*) *49*
**TSHUMA** Loreen (ZIM, *2021-24*) *35*

## CONUNDRUM 197

Can you unscramble the anagram to reveal the name of a West Indies women's cricketer?

**THE GAMMON DINERS** (WI) (*15 WT20I's, 2019-23*)

## VARIATION 198

Can you complete the grid so that every row and column contain each of the letters found in the surname of Aimee **WATKINS** (NZ) (*103 WODI's, 2002-11*)?

| | | | | | | |
|---|---|---|---|---|---|---|
| | K | | | W | | I |
| | | | | | | |
| | A | | T | | K | |
| | | N | | I | | W |
| | S | | | | A | |
| A | | W | | | | |
| | N | | | S | | |

## DIRECTION 199

Taking a letter from each segment of the circle in turn, can you spell out the name of a women's national cricket team and the team's nickname (*8,8*). You need to find the starting points and identify the direction the names are spelt.

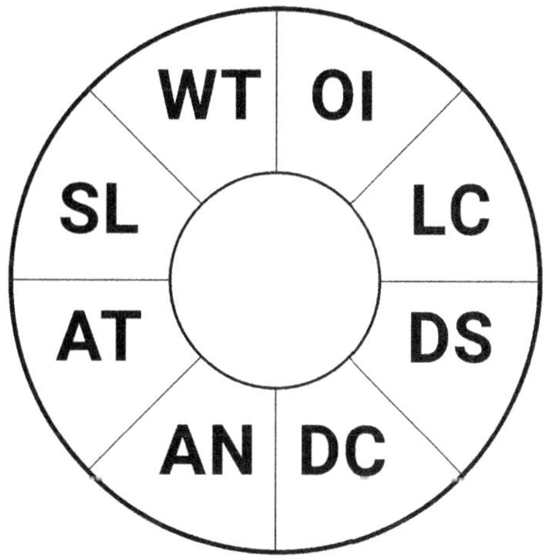


## TAILENDERS 200

The name of a Australia women's cricketer (*5 WT20I's, 2019*) can be inserted in the bottom row of the grid below to complete nine 3-letter words reading downwards. Can you identify them?

| | | | | | | | | |
|---|---|---|---|---|---|---|---|---|
| D | F | S | P | R | E | C | O | H |
| U | A | K | E | O | M | A | W | I |
| | | | | | | | | |

# SOLUTIONS

## 1 FIELDING POSITIONS

Extra cover, Long off, Square leg, Third man, Silly mid-on, Fly slip, Backward point, Deep mid-wicket, Cow corner, Straight hit

## 2 ROTATION

Jemimah Rodrigues

## 3 CRIDOKU

| Y | I | G | E | W | S | L | B | A |
|---|---|---|---|---|---|---|---|---|
| S | A | W | I | B | L | G | Y | E |
| B | E | L | G | A | Y | I | W | S |
| G | W | B | A | L | E | S | I | Y |
| L | S | E | B | Y | I | A | G | W |
| I | Y | A | S | G | W | B | E | L |
| A | G | Y | L | E | B | W | S | I |
| W | B | S | Y | I | A | E | L | G |
| E | L | I | W | S | G | Y | A | B |

## 4 CONNECTION

Bath, Court, Green, Post (surname is type of room); Malik, Meghana, Sokomanu, Yousaf (surname includes a country); Jones, Mooney, O'Neill, Stonell (surname includes the number one); Blackwell, Bryce, Joyce, Kerr (sister is also an international cricketer)

## 5 BUMP BALL

KLAAS: Mlaba, Bosch, Jafta, Lewis, Khaka

## 6 RECORD HOLDER

A. 11 years, 40 days

## 7 WORDSEARCH

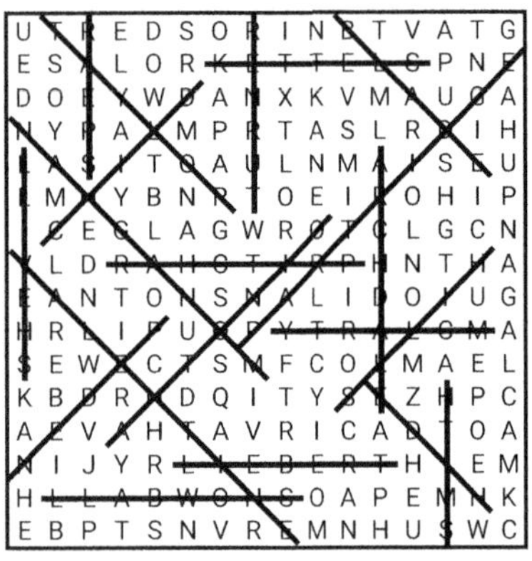

## 8 CRYPTOGRAM

STAFANIE TAYLOR: She has the ability to flick a switch and hit the ball wherever she wants.

## 9 HIT FOR SIX

| A | Y | P | S | E | C |
|---|---|---|---|---|---|
| E | C | A | Y | S | P |
| Y | S | C | A | P | E |
| C | P | Y | E | A | S |
| P | E | S | C | Y | A |
| S | A | E | P | C | Y |

## 10 BATTING ORDER

Udeshika Prabodhani

## 11 CRICKET CODEWORD

| P | L | A | S | T | I | C |  | H | E | L | L | O |
|---|---|---|---|---|---|---|---|---|---|---|---|---|
| R |  | N |  | H |  | A |  | Y |  | E |  | U |
| E | A | G | L | E |  | V | A | G | R | A | N | T |
| F |  | U |  | M |  | I |  | I |  | S |  | L |
| E | V | I | D | E | N | T |  | E | X | T | R | A |
| R |  | S |  |  |  | Y |  | N |  |  |  | W |
|  | W | H | I | T | E |  | F | E | R | N | S |  |
| J |  |  |  | R |  | C |  |  |  | O |  | S |
| A | I | S | L | E |  | A | B | D | O | M | E | N |
| C |  | Q |  | K |  | M |  | E |  | A |  | E |
| K | N | U | C | K | L | E |  | B | A | D | G | E |
| A |  | A |  | E |  | R |  | U |  | I |  | Z |
| L | A | T | E | R |  | A | R | T | I | C | L | E |

## 12 CONUNDRUM

Nigar Sultana

## 13 CROSS OVER

```
B                           D O T T I N
L   C     H O C K L E Y           I
A   L E E     H           B   W   F
C   A     B R O W N E   M A R O O F         S
K E R R       P       M   T   L   E     T   A
W   K   S H A R M A   C   E   V   N   R A U T
E       C     A       G   S   A         Y   T
L A N N I N G   R O L L S   K A U R     L   E
L       V   R   A     A   K   R         O   R
    L   E   E   J     S   A   D         R   T
  D U P R E E Z   A T H A P A T H T H U     H
    U   B   N   B     A   P     E       V   W
    S I R I W A R D E N E     M A N D H A N A
        U   A   I   D       S   L       N   I
  M O O N E Y   T   W   B   H   Y   P   N   T
  A     T     S T H A L E K A R   D E V I N E
  T             I   R   A   R       R   E
  T A Y L O R   N   D R U M M   C   R   K
  H         O       S   M   A   H A Y N E S
K E I G H T L E Y       O       E       R
  W         T     K H A N   N I T S C H K E
  S         O           T       T
          K N I G H T       T A Y L O R
```

## 14 STEPLADDER

JANE, LANE, LAND, LAID, SAID, SLID, SLIT, SMIT

## 15 BRAINTEASER

6: If you consider that the cricketers who didn't play in each of the formats was different in each case (ie. 8 in Tests, 3 in ODI's and 5 in T20I's = 16) it leaves 6 cricketers who must have played in all 3 formats

## 16 LOGIC PUZZLE

Agnes, 2nd slip, 35 caps, Victoria; Harriet, 3rd slip, 8 caps, Western Australia; Martha, wicket-keeper, 64 caps, Tasmania; Zoe, 1st slip, 21 caps, New South Wales

## 17 WAGON WHEEL

(9) Riverside
(8) Derisive
(7) Deriver, desirer, deviser, diverse, redrive, resider, reversi, revised, reviser, rivered, riviere, serried
(6) Derive, desire, driver, irised, reived, reiver, rerise, reside, revied, revise, rieved, riever, serred, served, server, sirred, sirree, verier, versed, verser, visier
(5) Direr, dreer, drere, drier, drive, eider, erred, reird, reive, resid, revie, rider, rieve, riser, rived, river, seder, sered, serer, serre, serve, sever, sider, sired, siree, siver, verse, vired, virid
(4) Deer, dere, derv, dire, dree, ered, erev, ever, ired, irid, rede, reed, ride, rise, rive, seer, seir, sere, serr, sire, siri, veer, verd, vier, vire

## 18 PATHFINDER

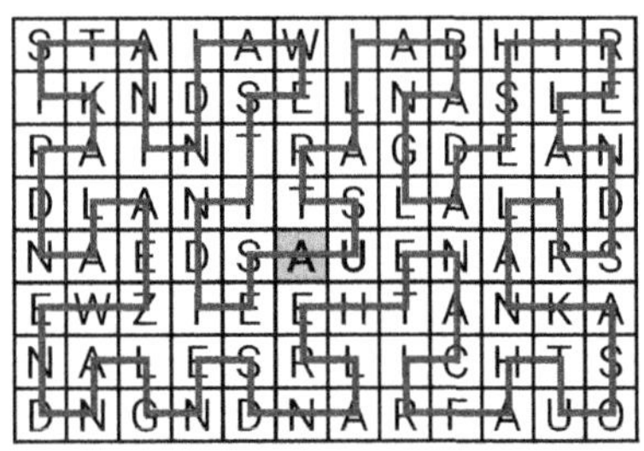

## 19 SCORECARD

Nida Dar 44, Iram Javed 30; Runs scored are calculated by multiplying the position in the alphabet of the first letter of the batter's last name with that of the bowler who took their wicket, eg. 4 (Nida Dar) x 11 (Arelene Kelly) = 44

# SOLUTIONS

## 20 MIDDLE ORDER

| | | | | |
|---|---|---|---|---|
| | R | W | C | |
| D | I | A | L | S |
| O | N | I | O | N |
| I | S | S | U | E |
| | E | T | D | |

## 21 FOURS

Lauren DOWN

## 22 MIXED UP PAIRS

Natalia Pervaiz

## 23 PITCH IT UP

GRACE HARRIS, Australia, UP Warriorz, Brisbane Heat, Queensland, London Spirit

## 24 DINGBATS

Nervous nineties, Green top

## 25 CRICKET CROSSWORD

| | | | | | | | | | | | | |
|---|---|---|---|---|---|---|---|---|---|---|---|---|
| | N | O | N | S | T | R | I | K | E | R | | |
| | | T | | T | | A | | H | | E | | D |
| D | H | A | K | A | | C | H | A | R | L | I | E |
| A | | G | | F | | H | | N | | E | | A |
| T | W | O | | A | L | E | X | | R | A | I | N |
| E | | | | N | | L | | M | | S | | |
| S | P | I | R | I | T | | S | A | X | E | N | A |
| | | N | | E | | S | | L | | | | V |
| F | I | N | E | | N | I | D | A | | D | A | R |
| A | | I | | R | | N | | Y | | R | | I |
| L | A | N | N | I | N | G | | S | P | I | L | L |
| L | | G | | A | | L | | I | | V | | |
| | | S | U | Z | I | E | B | A | T | E | S | |

## 26 VARIATION

| | | | | | | |
|---|---|---|---|---|---|---|
| O | I | G | A | M | S | W |
| M | G | I | W | A | O | S |
| I | S | W | G | O | A | M |
| A | M | S | O | I | W | G |
| S | W | O | M | G | I | A |
| G | O | A | S | W | M | I |
| W | A | M | I | S | G | O |

## 27 MID-OFF

Tazmin Brits

## 28 STAIRCASE

| | | | | | | |
|---|---|---|---|---|---|---|
| G | O | R | D | O | N | |
| L | A | N | N | I | N | G |
| | P | R | I | C | E | |
| K | E | N | D | A | L | L |
| | B | U | R | N | S | |
| L | U | M | S | D | E | N |
| | H | U | N | T | E | R |

## 29 ICC HALL OF FAME

2010 Rachael Heyhoe-Flint, 2011 Belinda Clark, 2012 Enid Bakewell, 2014 Debbie Hockley, 2015 Betty Wilson, 2016 Karen Rolton, 2018 Caire Taylor, 2019 Cathryn Fitzpatrick, 2020 Lisa Sthalekar, 2021 Jan Brittin, 2022 Charlotte Edwards, 2023 Diana Edulji, 2024 Neetu David

## 30 MISSING LETTERS

Fahima Khatun

## 31 HIT FOR SIX

| | | | | | |
|---|---|---|---|---|---|
| Y | L | E | D | A | N |
| A | E | Y | N | D | L |
| N | D | L | Y | E | A |
| D | A | N | L | Y | E |
| F | N | D | A | I | Y |
| L | Y | A | E | N | D |

## 32 WORDSEARCH

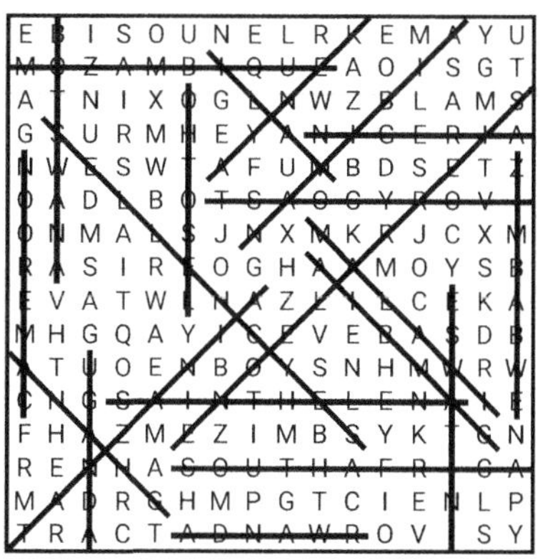

1. BOTSWANA, 2. CAMEROON, 3. ESWATINI, 4. GAMBIA, 5. GHANA, 6. IVORY COAST, 7. KENYA, 8. LESOTHO, 9. MALAWI, 10. MALI, 11. MOZAMBIQUE, 12. NAMIBIA, 13. NIGERIA, 14. RWANDA, 15. SAINT HELENA, 16. SEYCHELLES, 17. SIERRA LEONE, 18. SOUTH AFRICA, 19. TANZANIA, 20. UGANDA, 21. ZIMBABWE

## 33 CRICTETRIS

| | | | | | |
|---|---|---|---|---|---|
| L | A | V | I | N | E |
| S | M | A | R | T | T |
| C | O | O | P | E | R |
| N | A | T | I | O | N |
| G | E | O | R | G | E |
| J | O | S | E | P | H |
| S | E | L | M | A | N |
| K | N | I | G | H | T |
| F | R | A | S | E | R |
| M | U | N | R | O | E |

## 34 TAILENDERS

Freya Kemp

## 35 INSIDE OUT

| | | | | | | |
|---|---|---|---|---|---|---|
| W | E | B | S | I | T | E |
| A | M | A | T | E | U | R |
| C | O | L | O | N | E | L |
| G | A | S | K | E | T | S |
| B | O | R | E | D | O | M |
| A | T | H | L | E | T | E |
| L | O | W | L | A | N | D |

## 36 DIRECTION

NEWLANDS, CAPE TOWN

## 37 CONUNDRUM

Georgia Plimmer

## 38 BUMP BALL

Ailsa LISTER: Carter, Spence, Rainey, Willis, Slater, Galvin

## 39 FIVE DOWN

Richa Ghosh

## 40 SILHOUETTE

Sarah Bryce, Shafali Verma, Mignon du Preez

# SOLUTIONS

## 41 CRIDOKU

| N | Y | A | K | S | C | I | W | H |
|---|---|---|---|---|---|---|---|---|
| H | C | S | I | A | W | N | K | Y |
| W | K | I | H | N | Y | S | C | A |
| I | H | C | N | K | A | W | Y | S |
| A | W | K | C | Y | S | H | I | N |
| S | N | Y | W | I | H | K | A | C |
| Y | I | N | A | H | K | C | S | W |
| C | A | H | S | W | I | Y | N | K |
| K | S | W | Y | C | N | A | H | I |

## 42 DO YOU KNOW?

B. England

## 43 CRICKET CIRCLES

Lauren CHEATLE, Sarah ELLIOTT, Rene FARRELL: AUSTRALIA

## 44 FOLLOW ON

| F | L | S | I | G | E | L | U | F | Y |
|---|---|---|---|---|---|---|---|---|---|
| I | A | I | A | W | A | R | D | R | A |
| N | T | T | R | O | H | P | U | A | L |
| I | E | R | I | A | L | B | E | O | P |
| S | P | E | A | M | R | U | L | B | I |
| H | I | S | C | E | A | N | I | Y | U |
| E | C | S | T | O | R | S | G | E | Q |
| R | H | N | I | F | F | R | A | K | E |
| O | A | I | R | E | T | H | I | N | D |
| C | C | U | P | I | E | D | E | C | A |

## 45 CROSSWORD 4s

| S | L | I | P | | B | A | L | L |
|---|---|---|---|---|---|---|---|---|
| | I | | A | | Y | | | |
| | N | | D | E | E | P | | N |
| N | E | T | S | | S | A | V | E |
| I | | O | | | | T | | X |
| C | L | U | B | | S | H | O | T |
| K | | R | E | S | T | | V | |
| | | | A | | E | | A | |
| W | A | I | T | | P | U | L | L |

## 46 BOX CLEVER

7,805: Mithali Raj is the leading runscorer in WODI's with 7,805 runs

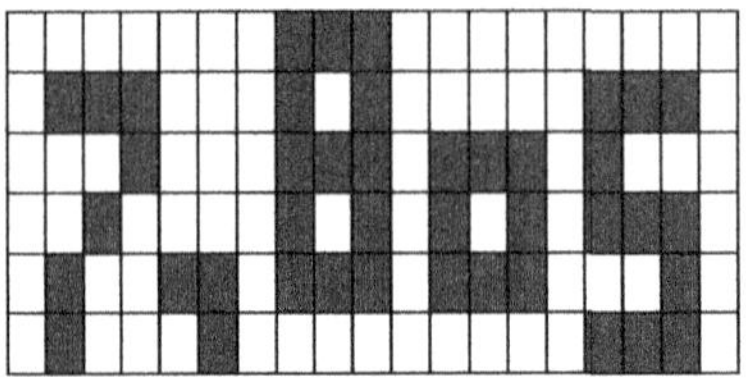

## 47 ODD ONE OUT

C: Ellyse Perry has never captained the national team

## 48 PARTNERSHIP

SERBIA: Lorna JACK, Juliet POST, Joyce BATH, Glenys PAGE, Mariko HILL, Melissa FARE

## 49 SIXERS

| 3 | 2 | 4 | 6 | 1 | 5 |
|---|---|---|---|---|---|
| 6 | 3 | 1 | 5 | 2 | 4 |
| 4 | 6 | 3 | 2 | 5 | 1 |
| 5 | 1 | 6 | 3 | 4 | 2 |
| 1 | 5 | 2 | 4 | 6 | 3 |
| 2 | 4 | 5 | 1 | 3 | 6 |

## 50 INSIDE OUT

| P | A | D | D | O | C | K |
|---|---|---|---|---|---|---|
| C | A | R | A | M | E | L |
| W | H | I | S | T | L | E |
| S | T | E | W | A | R | D |
| C | E | R | A | M | I | C |
| P | E | A | N | U | T | S |
| S | A | L | I | E | N | T |

## 51 ROTATION

Sachini Nisansala

## 52 WORDSEARCH

1. CHRISTCHURCH, 2. PEARLS, 3. THE VILLAGE, 4. GLASGOW, 5. TREDREA, 6. UGANDA, 7. LION, 8. MAHIKA GAUR, 9. MINX, 10. BANGLADESH, 11. INDIA, 12. KIM COTTON, 13. SMITHIES, 14. WHITE HEATHER, 15. SOUTH AFRICA

## 52 WORDSEARCH (cont.)

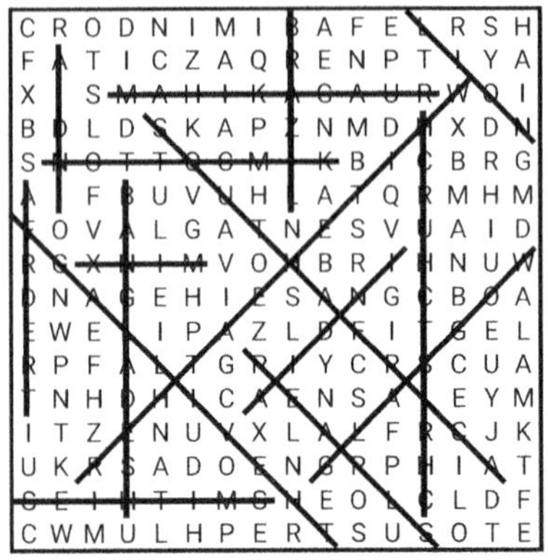

## 53 MISSING LETTERS

Kathryn Bryce

## 54 MIDDLE ORDER

| | A | P | G | |
|---|---|---|---|---|
| S | M | A | R | T |
| F | I | N | A | L |
| A | S | I | D | E |
| | S | C | E | |

## 55 ICC MEMBERS

Ireland, Costa Rica, Romania, Australia, Botswana, Eswatini, Malaysia: NAMIBIA

## 56 RUNS TEASER

BHOGLE 32, CHUDASAMA 17, DHINGRA 21, KOLAN 45, SRIHARSHA 6

## 57 VARIATION

| U | O | B | S | R | E | L |
|---|---|---|---|---|---|---|
| E | U | R | L | S | O | B |
| B | L | S | E | O | R | U |
| L | B | U | O | E | S | R |
| R | S | O | U | B | L | E |
| S | R | E | B | L | U | O |
| O | E | L | R | U | B | S |

## 58 SIX DOWN

Louise Browne

## 59 CONUNDRUM

Ciara Metcalfe

# SOLUTIONS

## 60 SQUARE CUT

Deepti Sharma

| | | | | | | | | |
|---|---|---|---|---|---|---|---|---|
| | T | | | I | | | S | |
| P | | M | E | | O | R | | H |
| | B | | | D | | | A | |
| | Y | | | O | | | S | |
| E | | O | N | | U | P | | A |
| | A | | | B | | | I | |
| | S | | | E | | | T | |
| E | | I | T | | W | E | | R |
| | D | | | A | | | M | |

## 61 MIXED UP 3's

Shashikala Siriwardene

## 62 WHO PLAYS WHO?

South Africa v Pakistan; New Zealand v England; West Indies v India; Sri Lanka v Australia

## 63 NAME BOGGLER

Sarah ALEY, Jess CAMERON, Nicola CAREY, Kim GARTH, Heather GRAHAM, Julie HAYES, Rachael HAYNES, Olivia MAGNO, Tahlia MCGRATH, Georgia WAREHAM

## 64 MISSING VOWELS

1. Bat and pad catch, 2. Hit the ball twice, 3. Incoming batter, 4. Ten wicket haul, 5. Bowled through the gate, 6. Hold up an end, 7. Unplayable delivery, 8. Farm the strike, 9. Batting for a draw, 10. Occupying the crease

## 65 OUTSIDE EDGE

Sripali WEERAKKODY, Freya SARGENT, Sarah ELLIOTT, Caroline SALOMONS, Marina LAMPLOUGH, Henao THOMAS, Elizabeth AKEHURST, Shaila SHARMIN, Reema MALHOTRA, Peggy FAIRWEATHER

## 66 CRICKET UMPIRES

KIM COTTON New Zealand, MARY WALDRON Ireland, SALEEMA IMTIAZ Pakistan, ANNA HARRIS England, CLAIRE POLOSAK Australia, SHIVAM MISHRA India, LAUREN AGENBAG South Africa

## 67 CONNECTION

All the player's names contain each of the 5 vowels in the English alphabet, and only once.

## 68 JUMBO CODEWORD

| | | | | | | | | | | | | |
|---|---|---|---|---|---|---|---|---|---|---|---|---|
| P | R | O | V | O | K | E | | S | P | O | O | K |
| | E | | A | | N | | S | | A | | V | |
| S | O | U | R | C | E | | H | U | N | T | E | R |
| | R | | N | | E | | R | | | | R | |
| A | D | M | I | T | | Q | U | I | P | P | E | D |
| | E | | S | | F | | B | | R | | G | |
| O | R | C | H | A | R | D | | K | I | N | G | |
| | | | E | | E | | A | | C | | | |
| H | E | A | D | W | E | A | R | | E | A | S | Y |
| | G | | | | Z | | C | | | | E | |
| Z | O | O | M | | E | X | H | I | B | I | T | S |
| | | | A | | R | | A | | L | | | |
| | G | U | S | T | | G | I | R | A | F | F | E |
| | L | | O | | H | | C | | M | | E | |
| R | A | I | N | B | O | W | | J | E | L | L | Y |
| | C | | | | I | | P | | L | | L | |
| F | I | E | L | D | S | | I | C | E | B | O | X |
| | A | | I | | T | | K | | S | | W | |
| B | L | A | D | E | | P | E | R | S | I | S | T |

## 69 STAIRCASE

| | | | | | | |
|---|---|---|---|---|---|---|
| H | O | L | D | E | N | |
| D | A | N | I | E | L | S |
| B | I | R | C | H | | |
| G | O | A | T | M | A | N |
| | | W | I | L | K | S |
| P | L | I | M | M | E | R |
| | G | R | U | N | D | Y |

## 70 BUMP BALL

Helen WATSON: Jensen, Browne, Turner, Mackay, Curtis, Doolan

## 71 HIT FOR SIX

| | | | | | |
|---|---|---|---|---|---|
| N | A | V | Y | Z | L |
| L | Y | A | V | N | Z |
| Z | V | L | N | Y | A |
| Y | Z | N | A | L | V |
| A | L | Y | Z | V | N |
| V | N | Z | L | A | Y |

## 72 CRICKET CROSSWORD

| | | | | | | | | | | | | |
|---|---|---|---|---|---|---|---|---|---|---|---|---|
| S | | S | | T | | | G | R | A | C | E | |
| H | E | A | L | Y | | U | | A | | H | | S |
| O | | N | | P | U | N | A | M | R | A | U | T |
| T | E | A | | H | | D | | P | | S | | U |
| | | M | O | O | N | E | Y | | S | E | A | M |
| A | | I | | O | | R | | D | | | | P |
| S | T | R | I | N | G | | C | I | R | C | L | E |
| M | | | | S | | V | | A | | O | | D |
| A | S | H | A | | S | E | L | M | A | N | | |
| V | | O | | L | | R | | O | | N | E | T |
| I | S | L | E | O | F | M | A | N | | E | | A |
| A | | L | | S | | A | | D | E | L | M | I |
| | W | Y | A | T | T | | | S | | L | | L |

## 73 SIDE ON

Campbelle, Perera, Meshram, Ismail, Carroll, Broadfoot, Farrant, Newlove, Sohail, Penfold

## 74 DINGBATS

All out, Net run rate

## 75 CONUNDRUM

Tuba Hassan

## 76 RECORD HOLDER

C. 67 years, 24 days

## 77 BATTING ORDER

Cathryn Fitzpatrick

## 78 PATHFINDER

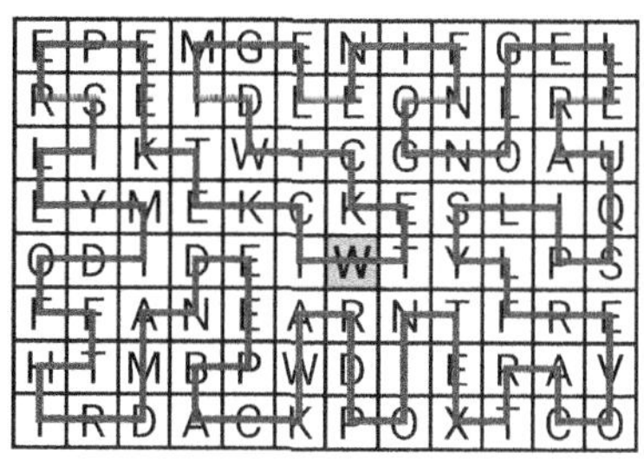

Fielding positions: Wicket-keeper, silly mid-off, third man, deep backward point, extra cover, fly slip, square leg, long on, fine leg, mid-wicket

# SOLUTIONS

## 79 CROSS OVER

## 80 STEPLADDER

LEAH, LEAD, LEND, LAND, LAID, PAID, PAIL, PAUL

## 81 PAIR UP

NO is unused; BELL, DEAN, GAUR, GUHA, LAMB, SMIT, WONG

## 82 CRIDOKU

| | | | | | | | | |
|---|---|---|---|---|---|---|---|---|
| T | I | W | E | H | G | N | S | M |
| H | E | N | M | S | W | G | I | T |
| S | G | M | T | I | N | E | W | H |
| M | N | E | I | T | S | H | G | W |
| W | S | H | G | N | M | T | E | I |
| G | T | I | W | E | H | M | N | S |
| I | W | G | H | M | E | S | T | N |
| N | M | T | S | G | I | W | H | E |
| E | H | S | N | W | T | I | M | G |

## 83 CRICKET CIRCLES

Moseline DANIELS, Nadine DE KLERK, Odine KIRSTEN: SOUTH AFRICA

## 84 MID-OFF

Lauren FILER

## 85 SILHOUETTE

Elyse Villani, Hayley Matthews, Shabnim Ismail

## 86 DIRECTION

Shaquana Quintyne

## 87 VARIATION

| | | | | | | |
|---|---|---|---|---|---|---|
| S | D | A | O | M | N | U |
| O | U | D | A | N | M | S |
| A | O | N | S | D | U | M |
| U | S | M | D | A | O | N |
| D | M | O | N | U | S | A |
| M | N | S | U | O | A | D |
| N | A | U | M | S | D | O |

## 88 MATCH UP

Gujarat Giants, India; Canterbury Magicians, New Zealand; Barbados Royals, West Indies; Lancashire Thunder, England; North West Dragons, South Africa; Perth Scorchers, Australia

## 89 BUMP BALL

Sarah FORBES: Boylan, O'Leary, Molins, Dawson, Coffey, Little

## 90 INSIDE OUT

| | | | | | | |
|---|---|---|---|---|---|---|
| A | B | S | C | O | N | D |
| E | M | P | A | T | H | Y |
| F | E | A | R | F | U | L |
| E | V | I | D | E | N | T |
| I | N | F | O | R | M | S |
| A | B | U | S | I | V | E |
| I | L | L | O | G | I | C |

## 91 CRICTETRIS

| | | | | | |
|---|---|---|---|---|---|
| G | I | B | S | O | N |
| E | L | W | I | S | S |
| G | O | R | D | O | N |
| A | T | K | I | N | S |
| N | E | W | T | O | N |
| D | A | V | I | E | S |
| C | O | N | N | O | R |
| H | A | Z | E | L | L |
| M | O | R | G | A | N |
| C | A | P | S | E | Y |

## 92 WORDSEARCH

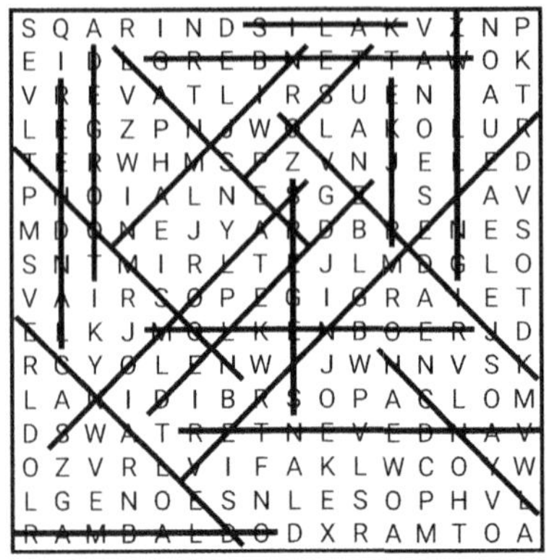

## 93 SURNAMES

ALANA KING: MARTIN, LEWIS, FRASER, GREEN, TAYLOR, KHAN, SMITH, HUNTER, SINGH

## 94 MISSING LETTERS

Nashra Sandhu

## 95 FIVE DOWN

KERRI LAING

## 96 END TO END RUN

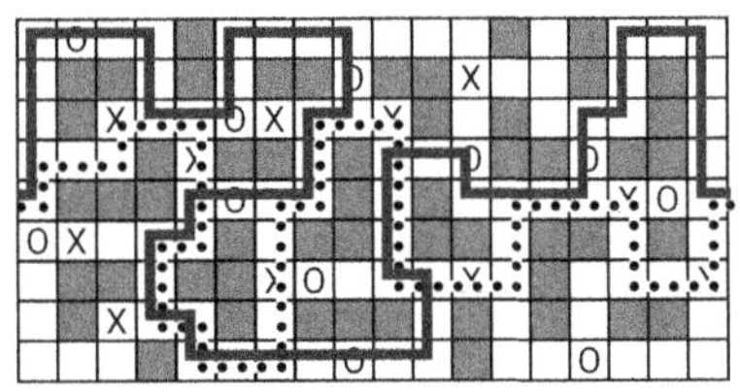

## 97 DO YOU KNOW?

A. Bahamas

## 98 CONNECTION

All the player's surnames contain a cricket-related term.

## 99 CONUNDRUM

Caroline Atkins

## 100 LOGIC PUZZLE

Tammy Beaumont, caught, Ramharack, 61; Maia Bouchier, stumped, Fletcher, 102; Alice Capsey, bowled, Matthews, 47; Heather Knight, caught & bowled, Connell, 3; Nat Sciver-Brunt, LBW, James, 29

# SOLUTIONS

## 101 WAGON WHEEL

(9) Technique
(7) Chutnee, quieten, quinche
(6) Chenet, cheque, cinque, entice, equine, ethnic, queint, quench, quetch, quethe, quiche, quince, quinte, techie, theine, thence
(5) Centu, chine, chute, ctene, cunei, cutie, ethic, ethne, hence, niche, niece, queen, quiet, quine, quite, tench, tenue, teuch, theic, thein, thine, uneth, unite, untie
(4) Cent, cete, cine, cite, cute, eche, echt, eech, eine, etch, eten, ethe, etic, etui, hent, hete, nete, nice, nite, tech, teen, tein, tene, thee, then, tice, tine, tune, unce

## 102 CRYPTOGRAM

KRISTEN BEAMS: If he's good at sport, he hopefully plays for Australia and if he's not, then he can play for England.

## 103 MIXED UP PAIRS

Kavisha Egodage

## 104 DINGBATS

Change of ends, Flat pitch

## 105 TAILENDERS

Sadia Butt

## 106 PITCH IT UP

RACHEL PRIEST, New Zealand, Central Districts, Trent Rockets, Hobart Hurricanes, Tasmania

## 107 MISSING LETTERS

Taniya Bhatia

## 108 RECORD HOLDER

C. 232 not out

## 109 CRICKET CODEWORD

| | | | | | | | | | | | | |
|---|---|---|---|---|---|---|---|---|---|---|---|---|
| A | P | L | O | M | B | | R | E | F | U | N | D |
| I | | I | | O | | S | | X | | N | | E |
| R | A | V | I | O | L | I | | C | L | I | M | B |
| F | | I | | N | | G | | A | | F | | T |
| L | A | D | Y | | C | H | E | V | R | O | N | S |
| O | | | | S | | T | | A | | R | | |
| W | I | C | K | E | D | | A | T | O | M | I | C |
| | | H | | A | | T | | E | | | | A |
| Q | U | E | S | T | I | O | N | | J | O | G | S |
| U | | A | | B | | X | | Z | | U | | C |
| A | P | P | L | E | | I | N | E | R | T | I | A |
| C | | E | | L | | C | | S | | D | | D |
| K | A | R | A | T | E | | S | T | R | O | K | E |

## 110 MIXED UP 3's

Alice Davidson-Richards

## 111 WORDSEARCH

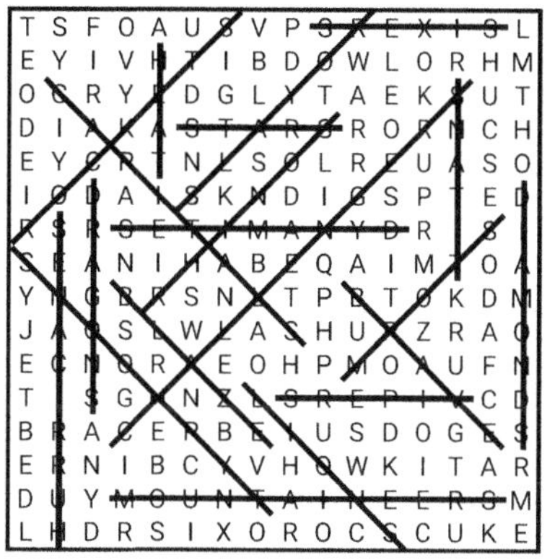

1. BLAZE, 2. BRAVE, 3. CAPITALS, 4. CHALLENGERS, 5. DIAMONDS, 6. DRAGONS, 7. DYNAMITES, 8. HEAT, 9. HURRICANES, 10. LIONS, 11. MOUNTAINEERS, 12. RHINOS,13. ROCKETS, 14. ROYALS, 15. SIXERS, 16. STARS, 17. STORM, 18. TITANS, 19. TYPHOONS, 20. VIPERS

## 112 CRICKET CIRCLES

Kate EBRAHIM, Debbie HOCKLEY, Lesley MURDOCH: NEW ZEALAND

## 113 MIDDLE ORDER

| | | | | |
|---|---|---|---|---|
| | T | H | S | |
| E | R | U | P | T |
| P | U | M | A | S |
| S | T | A | N | D |
| | H | N | S | |

## 114 PARTNERSHIP

LESOTHO: Maddy GREEN, Debra STOCK, Kathryn WHITE, Natasha MILES, Cliodhna SHARP, Stephanie POWER, Maryke SHORT

## 115 CROSSWORD 4s

| | | | | | | | | |
|---|---|---|---|---|---|---|---|---|
| M | | F | L | A | T | | | K |
| I | | | E | | E | D | G | E |
| S | | B | A | T | S | | | E |
| S | T | O | P | | T | R | A | P |
| | | W | | | | A | | |
| C | A | L | L | | T | I | E | S |
| O | | | O | P | E | N | | P |
| R | U | N | S | | A | | | I |
| K | | | T | I | M | E | | N |

## 116 BOX CLEVER

HOOF: Anya Shrubsole's nickname is Hoof.

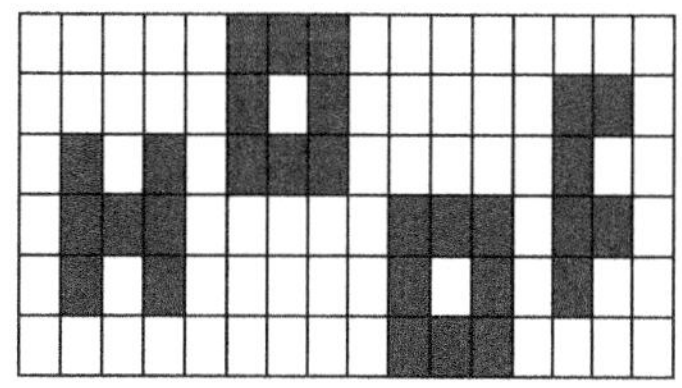

## 117 CRIDOKU

| | | | | | | | | |
|---|---|---|---|---|---|---|---|---|
| R | H | S | O | Y | W | B | A | N |
| N | A | Y | B | R | H | S | O | W |
| B | O | W | S | N | A | Y | R | H |
| A | S | H | N | B | O | W | Y | R |
| W | B | O | Y | A | R | N | H | S |
| Y | N | R | H | W | S | O | B | A |
| S | Y | B | R | H | N | A | W | O |
| O | R | A | W | S | B | H | N | Y |
| H | W | N | A | O | Y | R | S | B |

## 118 SIX DOWN

Ayesha Naseem

## 119 ROTATION

Eimear Richardson

## 120 FOURS

Danielle SMALL

## 121 HIT FOR SIX

| | | | | | |
|---|---|---|---|---|---|
| A | H | E | Y | S | N |
| S | E | Y | H | N | A |
| H | S | N | E | A | Y |
| Y | N | H | A | E | S |
| N | Y | A | S | H | E |
| E | A | S | N | Y | H |

# SOLUTIONS

## 122 TWINS

Alex & Kate Blackwell, Australia; Cecilia & Isobel Joyce, Ireland; Kycia & Kyshona Knight, West Indies;
Jane & Jill Powell, England; Liz & Rose Signal, New Zealand

## 123 FOLLOW ON

| | | | | | | | | | |
|---|---|---|---|---|---|---|---|---|---|
| L | N | U | N | E | M | O | H | T | A |
| A | I | I | P | I | R | T | H | G | F |
| P | V | Z | C | I | W | T | N | I | F |
| T | E | Z | E | U | P | A | E | N | U |
| O | R | A | X | L | L | C | L | K | R |
| P | S | N | A | A | L | S | A | C | D |
| A | E | G | M | I | N | E | T | I | N |
| R | M | U | I | S | H | I | L | K | A |
| A | P | L | O | Y | S | I | D | E | D |
| M | O | U | N | T | H | U | M | B | E |

## 124 PAIR UP

QI is unused; AMIN, BAIG, KHAN, RAUF, RIAZ, SANA, SHAH

## 125 CRICKET (DING)BATS

Top order, Caught behind

## 126 CONUNDRUM

Darcie Brown

## 127 CRICKET CROSSWORD

| | | | | | | | | | | | | |
|---|---|---|---|---|---|---|---|---|---|---|---|---|
| T | U | S | K | E | R | S | | K | H | A | K | A |
| E | | H | | | | M | | I | | | | D |
| S | T | A | R | S | | R | U | N | R | A | T | E |
| T | | P | | T | | I | | G | | L | | L |
| | C | E | L | E | S | T | E | | | I | S | A |
| F | | | | R | | I | | C | | C | | I |
| U | M | P | I | R | E | | S | H | I | E | L | D |
| L | | R | | E | | B | | E | | | | E |
| L | A | I | | | W | E | S | T | E | R | N | |
| T | | Z | | B | | A | | T | | A | | O |
| O | V | E | R | A | R | M | | Y | A | D | A | V |
| S | | | | I | | E | | | | H | | A |
| S | W | I | N | G | | R | E | D | B | A | L | L |

## 128 MIDDLE ORDER

| | | | | |
|---|---|---|---|---|
| | R | K | M | |
| G | E | N | E | S |
| S | L | A | T | E |
| D | I | C | E | D |
| | C | K | R | |

## 129 MID-OFF

Shanel DALEY

## 130 ODD ONE OUT

B: Smriti Mandhana didn't score a century in her 2nd international match.
Amy Hunter of Ireland is the youngest-ever WODI centurion.

## 131 STAIRCASE

| | | | | | | |
|---|---|---|---|---|---|---|
| P | U | L | F | O | R | D |
| B | E | V | E | G | E | |
| | G | R | E | E | N | |
| H | O | C | K | L | E | Y |
| | L | E | W | I | S | |
| | B | R | O | W | N | E |
| S | C | R | I | P | P | S |

## 132 CRICKET GROUNDS

Eden Gardens, Kolkata; Buffalo Park, East London; Allan Border Field, Brisbane; New Road, Worcester, Gaddafi Stadium, Lahore; Castle Avenue, Dublin; Basin Reserve, Wellington; ICC Academy, Dubai; Sinhalese Sports Club, Colombo; Kensington Oval, Bridgetown

## 133 WORDSEARCH

| | | | | | | | | | | | | | | | |
|---|---|---|---|---|---|---|---|---|---|---|---|---|---|---|---|
| A | X | S | M | I | J | E | F | I | R | P | N | R | N | A | M |
| W | G | T | A | O | R | O | L | L | S | F | O | I | M | S | Q |
| J | A | U | N | H | W | T | N | A | I | L | V | W | I | P | C |
| C | H | E | T | A | M | R | J | E | Y | M | E | S | R | J | N |
| P | S | B | L | D | Z | A | W | A | N | A | R | D | I | S | A |
| R | A | D | A | G | U | M | T | J | I | D | N | A | E | H | R |
| I | S | M | I | T | P | A | U | S | T | O | E | M | L | V | O |
| E | G | A | L | J | O | N | R | I | R | J | S | C | L | E | B |
| S | J | M | F | D | A | O | M | D | A | E | K | A | I | N | A |
| T | W | R | T | I | L | D | L | I | M | S | H | Z | U | R | T |
| H | A | L | K | S | E | A | K | T | R | E | D | N | G | V | P |
| M | L | Y | N | J | W | R | O | L | A | J | H | L | A | H | S |
| O | A | B | A | T | O | A | C | H | E | T | T | Y | E | M | O |
| K | T | Y | S | I | T | M | I | B | P | R | L | A | J | I | N |
| J | A | I | N | R | W | A | L | S | E | U | L | M | S | Y | T |
| T | M | S | F | P | N | S | M | V | I | Y | O | T | A | B | I |

## 134 SIXERS

| | | | | | |
|---|---|---|---|---|---|
| 4 | 1 | 3 | 2 | 5 | 6 |
| 5 | 4 | 2 | 6 | 3 | 1 |
| 3 | 2 | 6 | 4 | 1 | 5 |
| 6 | 5 | 1 | 3 | 2 | 4 |
| 1 | 3 | 4 | 5 | 6 | 2 |
| 2 | 6 | 5 | 1 | 4 | 3 |

## 135 INSIDE OUT

| | | | | | | |
|---|---|---|---|---|---|---|
| C | L | I | M | A | T | E |
| V | A | C | A | N | C | Y |
| U | P | E | N | D | E | D |
| M | E | S | S | A | G | E |
| O | C | T | A | G | O | N |
| T | O | I | L | E | T | S |
| R | O | S | E | T | T | E |

## 136 DIRECTION

Margaret Jennings

## 137 VARIATION

| | | | | | | |
|---|---|---|---|---|---|---|
| K | Y | D | L | N | U | E |
| E | D | N | U | L | Y | K |
| L | U | K | Y | D | E | N |
| N | E | Y | D | U | K | L |
| U | L | E | K | Y | N | D |
| D | N | U | E | K | L | Y |
| Y | K | L | N | E | D | U |

## 138 BUMP BALL

Ekta BISHT: Ahuja, Sadhu, Punia, Dhrub, Patil

## 139 NAME BOGGLER

Muneeba ALI, Diana BAIG, Tazmin BRITS, Chinelle HENRY, Harmanpreet KAUR, Alana KING, Sugandika KUMARI, Rosemary MAIR, Hannah RAINEY, Shathi RANI, Renuka SINGH

## 140 SUPER CRICTETRIS

| | | | | | | | |
|---|---|---|---|---|---|---|---|
| M | A | N | O | D | A | R | A |
| B | E | A | U | M | O | N | T |
| H | A | L | L | I | D | A | Y |
| N | O | T | Z | A | K | H | E |
| G | A | Y | A | K | W | A | D |
| Z | W | I | L | L | I | N | G |
| U | R | Q | U | H | A | R | T |
| F | L | E | T | C | H | E | R |
| K | I | M | M | I | N | C | E |
| M | C | C | A | R | T | H | Y |

# SOLUTIONS

### 141 WHO PLAYS WHO?
Bangladesh v Scotland; Ireland v Thailand; Netherlands v PNG; UAE v Zimbabwe

### 142 CONNECTION
Carter, Ford, Taylor, Adams (same surname as former President of USA); Fourie, Hartenhof, Jones, Keightley (surname includes a number); Lean, Preez, Reilly, Silva (affix is missing from surname, ie. De Silva, Du Preez, McLean, O'Reilly); Devine, Ecclestone, MacMahon, Molineux (First name is Sophie - and not as shown in question)

### 143 PITCH IT UP
FRAN WILSON, England, Oval Invincibles, Western Storm, Sydney Thunder, Wellington Blaze

### 144 CROSS OVER

### 145 STEPLADDER
KARY, WARY, WARN, WORN, CORN, COIN, CHIN, CHAN

### 146 MIDDLE ORDER

| | | | | |
|---|---|---|---|---|
| | S | T | E | |
| W | H | A | L | E |
| R | E | B | E | L |
| F | L | O | C | K |
| | L | O | T | |

### 147 SILHOUETTE
Muneeba Ali, Danni Wyatt-Hodge, Stafanie Taylor

### 148 BATTING ORDER
Lauren Winfield-Hill

### 149 DO YOU KNOW?
D. Ireland

### 150 CONUNDRUM
Shreyanka Patil

### 151 SQUARE CUT
Bismah Maroof

| | | | | | | | | |
|---|---|---|---|---|---|---|---|---|
| | I | | | B | | | F | |
| S | | O | R | | A | T | | O |
| | M | | | H | | | A | |
| | Y | | | E | | | T | |
| M | | S | O | | U | S | | O |
| | I | | | N | | | B | |
| | N | | | O | | | Y | |
| A | | I | F | | W | E | | R |
| | H | | | M | | | A | |

### 152 MIXED UP PAIRS
Tayla Vlaeminck

### 153 FIVE DOWN
Maria Silva

### 154 MISSING LETTERS
Arran Brindle

### 155 ICC MEMBERS
Cambodia, Indonesia, Tanzania, Germany, Mongolia, Netherlands, Sri Lanka: DENMARK

### 156 WORDSEARCH

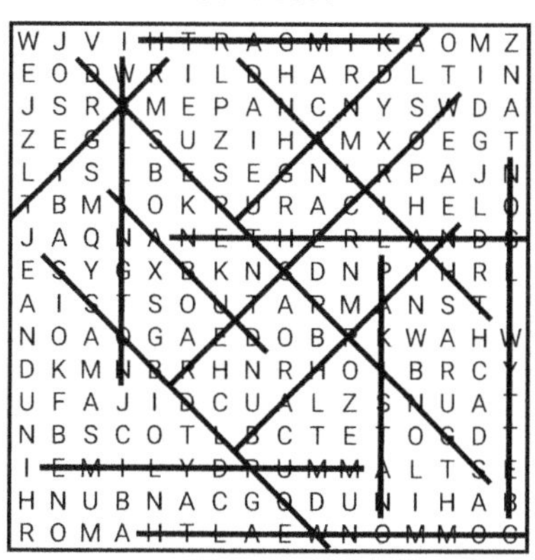

1. THAILAND, 2. COMMONWEALTH, 3. PAKISTAN, 4. EMILY DRUMM, 5. UGANDA, 6. DUBAI, 7. WORLD BOSS, 8. NETHERLANDS, 9. DESERT SPRINGS, 10. BETTY WILSON, 11. KIM GARTH, 12. TIGER, 13. WORCESTER, 14. BAHRAIN, 15. WELLINGTON

### 157 SIDE ON
Shrubsole, Maroof, Carson, Wareham, Tanwar, Dottin, Armstrong, Chipare, Sweetman, Goodall

### 158 SCORECARD
Puja Mahato 29, Kabita Joshi 21; Runs scored are calculated by adding together the positions in the alphabet of the first letter of each of the batter's name, eg. Puja Mahato is 16(P) + 13(M) = 29

### 159 CRIDOKU

| | | | | | | | | |
|---|---|---|---|---|---|---|---|---|
| O | B | U | E | L | R | S | J | Y |
| Y | S | E | B | J | O | U | L | R |
| R | J | L | Y | U | S | E | B | O |
| L | R | S | O | E | U | J | Y | B |
| E | O | Y | S | B | J | R | U | L |
| B | U | J | R | Y | L | O | S | E |
| S | L | B | J | R | E | Y | O | U |
| J | Y | R | U | O | B | L | E | S |
| U | E | O | L | S | Y | B | R | J |

### 160 INSIDE OUT

| | | | | | | |
|---|---|---|---|---|---|---|
| E | X | A | C | T | L | Y |
| A | N | T | H | E | M | S |
| S | T | E | A | L | T | H |
| C | A | B | I | N | E | T |
| P | R | O | W | E | S | S |
| L | O | C | A | T | E | D |
| A | D | M | I | R | E | R |

# SOLUTIONS

### 161 CRICKET UMPIRES

ELOISE SHERIDAN Australia, NIMALI PERERA Sri Lanka, SUE REDFERN England, JACQUELINE WILLIAMS West Indies, SARAH DAMBANEVANA Zimbabwe, KATHY CROSS New Zealand, VRINDA RATHI India

### 162 JUMBO CODEWORD

| | | | | | | | | | | | | |
|---|---|---|---|---|---|---|---|---|---|---|---|---|
| J | O | K | E | R | | T | H | U | N | D | E | R |
| | Z | | X | | C | | U | | I | | V | |
| P | O | T | T | E | R | | N | A | G | G | E | D |
| | N | | R | | O | | T | | H | | N | |
| H | E | R | O | I | S | M | | S | T | O | I | C |
| | | | V | | S | | S | | C | | N | |
| A | C | H | E | D | | A | P | O | L | O | G | Y |
| | O | | R | | A | | L | | U | | | |
| Q | U | I | T | | S | N | O | W | B | A | L | L |
| | R | | | | S | | D | | | | I | |
| S | T | A | R | L | I | N | G | | C | A | K | E |
| | | | E | | G | | E | | E | | E | |
| D | E | A | F | E | N | S | | M | A | R | S | H |
| | Y | | U | | S | | B | | S | | | |
| H | E | A | T | H | | J | U | K | E | B | O | X |
| | S | | A | | B | | L | | F | | T | |
| S | O | M | B | R | E | | K | N | I | G | H | T |
| | R | | L | | L | | Y | | R | | E | |
| R | E | V | E | A | L | S | | W | E | I | R | D |

### 163 CRICKETER OF THE YEAR

2012 & 14 Stafanie Taylor, 2013 & 16 Suzie Bates, 2015 Meg Lanning, 2017 Amy Satterthwaite, 2018 Smriti Mandhana, 2019 Ellyse Perry, 2021 Lizelle Lee, 2022 Nat Sciver-Brunt, 2023 Chamari Athapaththu

### 164 CRICKET CIRCLES

Alana DALZELL, Georgina DEMPSEY, Jane MAGUIRE: IRELAND

### 165 HIT FOR SIX

| | | | | | |
|---|---|---|---|---|---|
| A | R | N | I | T | M |
| M | N | A | T | R | I |
| I | M | R | A | N | T |
| R | I | T | M | A | N |
| T | A | M | N | I | R |
| N | T | I | R | M | A |

### 166 FOLLOW ON

| | | | | | | | | | |
|---|---|---|---|---|---|---|---|---|---|
| Q | T | P | A | R | E | G | A | N | E |
| U | U | K | C | A | R | T | E | C | E |
| I | R | E | H | S | I | N | I | A | T |
| B | O | L | E | U | T | R | M | R | R |
| B | U | P | C | N | P | E | I | A | U |
| L | S | R | T | A | S | V | D | E | G |
| E | C | O | I | C | U | L | N | L | O |
| M | R | L | O | N | G | R | A | C | Y |
| O | U | B | U | R | E | A | U | N | R |
| J | I | T | C | H | E | R | A | L | D |

### 167 NATIONALITY

Lucia Taylor ARGENTINA, Deepika Rasangika SRI LANKA, Rubina Chhetry NEPAL, Harmanpreet Kaur INDIA, Deandra Dottin WEST INDIES, Rita Musmali UGANDA, Grace Wetherall JERSEY, Andrea-Mae Zepeda AUSTRIA, Anneri van Schoor NAMIBIA, Florence Agaimalo SAMOA

### 168 PAIR UP

SI is unused; DEOL, DHAR, JAIN, KALA, MANI, NAIK, RAUT

### 169 STAIRCASE

| | | | | | | |
|---|---|---|---|---|---|---|
| A | T | K | I | N | S | |
| G | L | A | S | G | O | W |
| | | L | E | W | I | S |
| | G | R | E | G | G | |
| D | A | L | E | Y | | |
| E | T | I | E | N | N | E |
| | M | U | N | R | O | E |

### 170 MID-OFF

Aiman ANWER

### 171 VARIATION

| | | | | | | |
|---|---|---|---|---|---|---|
| R | S | O | T | A | Y | M |
| T | M | Y | R | S | A | O |
| S | A | R | M | T | O | Y |
| Y | O | A | S | R | M | T |
| M | R | T | O | Y | S | A |
| A | T | M | Y | O | R | S |
| O | Y | S | A | M | T | R |

### 172 MATCH UP

Guyana Amazon Warriors, West Indies; Birmingham Phoenix, England; Brisbane Heat, Australia; Delhi Capitals, India; Western Province, South Africa; Auckland Hearts, New Zealand

### 173 PATHFINDER

| | | | | | | | | |
|---|---|---|---|---|---|---|---|---|
| E | R | M | S | W | A | L | I | Z |
| B | N | U | T | O | N | E | B | E |
| A | I | D | A | B | A | B | A | N |
| R | B | M | U | L | U | E | D | G |
| H | A | G | I | G | B | S | A | L |
| B | E | L | R | A | N | H | B | E |
| L | A | R | I | T | A | S | U | L |
| I | Z | B | A | U | H | B | R | A |

Teams: Bulgaria, Brazil, Belgium, Bahrain, Bermuda, Botswana, Belize, Bangladesh, ~~Belarus~~, Bhutan

### 174 OUTSIDE EDGE

Jemimah RODRIGUES, Annerie DERCKSEN, Abtaha MAQSOOD, Sylvia SHIHEPO, Theertha SATISH, Marianne HERBERT, Jiska HOWARD, Isani VAGHELA, Shamilia CONNELL, Mandie GODLIMAN

### 175 DINGBATS

Lower order, Spread the field

### 176 LOGIC PUZZLE

9, Amelia Kerr, LBW review, straight hit; 27, Rosemary Mair, dropped catch, square cut; 58, Hannah Rowe, medical treatment, reverse sweep; 73, Fran Jonas, run out partner, cover drive; 106, Lea Tahuhu, shot of the day, leg glance

### 177 BATTING ORDER

Rajeshwari Gayakwad

### 178 SIX DOWN

RACHEL ANDREW

# SOLUTIONS

## 179 CROSSWORD 4s

| | | | | | | | | |
|---|---|---|---|---|---|---|---|---|
| P | | | L | O | O | P | | D |
| A | R | E | A | | V | | | U |
| I | | | T | I | E | D | | C |
| R | O | P | E | | R | I | S | K |
| | | O | | | | V | | |
| T | O | S | S | | H | E | A | D |
| A | | T | A | K | E | | | A |
| I | | | F | | L | O | S | S |
| L | | L | E | A | D | | | H |

## 180 ROTATION

Sophie Ecclestone

## 181 INSIDE OUT

| | | | | | | |
|---|---|---|---|---|---|---|
| U | N | K | N | O | W | N |
| M | A | T | I | N | E | E |
| B | E | N | E | A | T | H |
| V | I | L | L | A | G | E |
| R | A | N | S | A | C | K |
| G | E | N | E | T | I | C |
| A | B | A | N | D | O | N |

## 182 PITCH IT UP

CHLOE TRYON, South Africa, Barbados Royals, Sydney Sixers, Central Guateng, Mumbai Indians

## 183 SUPER CRICTETRIS

| | | | | | | | |
|---|---|---|---|---|---|---|---|
| L | E | T | S | O | A | L | O |
| V | I | L | L | I | E | R | S |
| Q | U | I | N | T | Y | N | E |
| A | N | D | E | R | S | O | N |
| Z | U | L | F | I | Q | A | R |
| K | A | V | A | N | A | G | H |
| N | I | T | S | C | H | K | E |
| M | A | N | D | H | A | N | A |
| F | O | E | R | S | T | E | R |
| K | A | S | P | E | R | A | K |

## 184 BRAINTEASER

Sri Lanka won the match by 1 run.

## 185 MIDDLE ORDER

| | | | | |
|---|---|---|---|---|
| | B | N | O | |
| L | E | A | V | E |
| R | E | S | E | T |
| S | C | A | R | F |
| | H | L | S | |

## 186 BUMP BALL

Lauren EBSARY: Haynes, Strano, Reeler, Jacobs, Schutt, Cooper

## 187 MIXED UP 3's

Nannapat Koncharoenkai

## 188 CROSS OVER

```
M   H I L L
U     A   G           A N D R E W
S U L T A N A   O   Z         Y
A   E   N   H U N T E R     I S H I M W E
M   W   I   G   P   G H
A L I   K N I G H T   E   B A H A D U R   K
L   S   G         D   L   O     A
I       R   C       A T H A P A T H T H U
  A G A T H A     C   A   N   T     R
K     S   H   H E A L Y   W   I   W
A   B L A K E       S   L   M O O N E Y   V
L E E   N   T   D   T   O   L     A   A
I   A N G G R A E N I   R   V   B A T E S
S   U   I   Y   V   N   K   A       T   Q
    M   K     B I M E N Y I M A N A       U
    O Z A   F   N   I     B   R     A B E L
    N       R   E   R O N A L D S     L   Z
    T       I       A     S   T       A
      M A T T H E W S     U           K
            Z                     H O Q U E
```

## 189 STEPLADDER

SIAN, SWAN, SWAP, SOAP, SOAK, SOCK, ROCK, RUCK

## 190 FOURS

Miriam KNEE

## 191 MISSING LETTERS

Nicole Bolton

## 192 CRIDOKU

| | | | | | | | | |
|---|---|---|---|---|---|---|---|---|
| U | Y | A | M | T | E | N | R | H |
| M | R | N | H | Y | A | E | U | T |
| E | H | T | R | N | U | Y | A | M |
| T | E | R | Y | A | H | M | N | U |
| H | N | U | E | R | M | T | Y | A |
| A | M | Y | N | U | T | H | E | R |
| R | T | M | A | E | Y | U | H | N |
| N | U | E | T | H | R | A | M | Y |
| Y | A | H | U | M | N | R | T | E |

## 193 HIT FOR SIX

| | | | | | |
|---|---|---|---|---|---|
| D | N | A | Y | E | P |
| E | Y | P | N | D | A |
| N | E | Y | A | P | D |
| A | D | E | P | N | Y |
| P | A | N | D | Y | E |
| Y | P | D | E | A | N |

## 194 RECORD HOLDER

B. 12.53

## 195 CRICKET CROSSWORD

| | | | | | | | | | | | | |
|---|---|---|---|---|---|---|---|---|---|---|---|---|
| | B | L | A | Z | E | | L | E | A | G | U | E |
| M | | E | | | S | | U | | | E | | D |
| A | L | A | M | | H | O | N | G | K | O | N | G |
| Q | | V | | | A | | C | | | R | | E |
| S | P | E | L | L | | C | H | A | R | G | E | |
| O | | | | E | | R | | S | | G | | V |
| O | Z | A | | G | H | O | S | H | | A | L | I |
| D | | M | | A | | S | | E | | | | L |
| | E | A | G | L | E | S | | S | K | I | L | L |
| L | | T | | | X | | O | | | N | | A |
| O | V | E | R | S | T | E | P | | E | D | E | N |
| O | | U | | | R | | E | | | I | | I |
| P | E | R | E | R | A | | N | I | G | A | R | |

## 196 WORDSEARCH

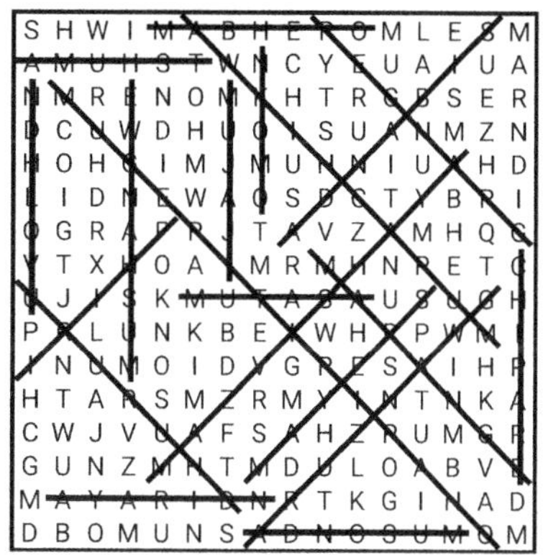

## 197 CONUNDRUM

Sheneta Grimmond

## 198 VARIATION

| | | | | | | |
|---|---|---|---|---|---|---|
| S | K | A | N | W | T | I |
| N | W | S | K | A | I | T |
| W | A | I | T | N | K | S |
| K | T | N | A | I | S | W |
| I | S | T | W | K | A | N |
| A | I | W | S | T | N | K |
| T | N | K | I | S | W | A |

## 199 DIRECTION

SCOTLAND / WILDCATS

## 200 TAILENDERS

Erin Burns

# FINAL WORD

Thank you for tackling *STUMPED Women's Cricket Puzzles* - I hope you had lots of fun solving the puzzles and that they provided just the right level of challenge.

If you have any comments or feedback on the puzzles, please get in touch. You can contact me at **info@stumpedcricket.com** – I'd love to hear from you.

Well done if you were able to solve the question in the Introduction relating to the image on the front cover. The three teams that have yet to play a Women's Test match are Bangladesh, Scotland and Zimbabwe.

# OTHER PUZZLE BOOKS

If you enjoyed the puzzles and word games then you'll be delighted to learn that a second collection is planned for publication in 2025. Yes, ***STUMPED Women's Cricket Puzzles Book 2*** will soon be available.

You might also be interested in *STUMPED Book of Cricket Puzzles* - which is a fantastic collection of 150 puzzles and word games on men's international cricket. And, you can always follow me on social media and have a go at solving the daily cricket puzzles.

# ACKNOWLEDGEMENTS

My biggest thanks must go to the cricketers who feature in this book. After all, the book would not have been possible without their achievements and contributions to the world of women's cricket.

I would also like to thank my partner, Suzanne. Despite being neither a cricket fan nor a puzzler, her love, support and overall contribution to *STUMPED* has been invaluable. Finally, my thanks to the star of the team, Pippa, our beautiful pet labrador, for helping to devise the puzzles and chilling out with me.

*Stephen Hearn*

Printed in Great Britain
by Amazon

60647475R00060